Contents

Beat Stress with CBT

Stephen Palmer and Christine Wilding

Hodder Education

338 Euston Road, London NW1 3BH

Hodder Education is an Hachette UK company

First published in UK 2011 by Hodder Education

This edition published 2011

www.hoddereducation.co.uk

Typeset by Cenveo Publisher Services

Printed in Great Britain by CPI Cox & Wyman, Reading

*To Maggie, Kate, Kevin, Tom, Arina, Josh, Sam, Harry and Aniket, who
have all helped me at different times to manage my stress. Stephen*

*For Frank, whose warmth, kindness and constant support have changed
my life immeasurably. Christine*

Meet the authors

Welcome to *Beat Stress with CBT*!

Most of us get stressed at some time in our lives. We may find daily life frustrating and stressful, too. Just travelling to work can be really irritating or using a computer that freezes or crashes can trigger rage. If we let it, stress can become debilitating. You may think that stress management just involves taking a jog or doing a bit of meditation. Of course, both activities may help us to unwind and relax, which is very useful. However, our view is: why get wound up in the first place? This is a question that this book examines and using our stress-busting thinking skills you will learn not only how to reduce stress but also how to prevent it, too, and even perform better at work, college and in social situations.

As a coaching and counselling psychologist [Stephen Palmer] and a psychotherapist [Christine Wilding], we work with people and organizations that suffer from stress triggered by overwork, demanding bosses and lack of time. On the home front, our clients may be stressed by relationship difficulties, unemployment and other live events. But it is how people deal with minor and major adversity that largely determines how stressed they become.

As professionally qualified practitioners, our job is to facilitate a person's own resources to troubleshoot the problems and develop solutions, thereby reducing or eliminating stress. Like other skills, the techniques and strategies can be learned and applied, and in this book we would like to share them with you.

Stephen Palmer and Christine Wilding

In one minute

We all recognize the feeling of being 'stressed out' – heart palpitations, frayed temper and clammy hands. But can we do anything about this? And anyway, isn't a little bit of stress good for us?

Well, no, stress is not good for us. It should not be confused with pressure, which is what motivates us to stretch ourselves both mentally and physically. Stress is completely different and ignoring it can lead to physical, psychological and social consequences that can all have damaging consequences for our wellbeing.

So, can we do anything about it? Well, the answer is 'yes'. First, we need to recognize what our own particular stressors are – people are stressed by different things. Perhaps it's letting a saucepan burn dry just as you are expecting your parents-in-law to arrive for lunch, or perhaps it's being asked to give a presentation to the Board of Directors. What might be a challenge to one person can be a stressor to another.

Once you identify what stresses you, then you can start to develop some stress-management strategies by creating your own personal 'de-stress tool box'. A good place to start is recognizing that how stressed you feel is more dependent on how you think about what happens, rather than what actually happens. Telling yourself something is 'awful' doesn't help lower your stress; it just elevates your stress levels.

Other useful tools include learning how to improve your communication and assertion skills, knock work stress on the head, relax, and cope with the stresses of parenting or personal relationships. Once you've learned how to use these tools, they will help you become more resilient and enjoy a more balanced, positive lifestyle.

Introduction

For some people, being under pressure is a way of life; they seem to thrive on it, at least in the short term. For others, too much pressure triggers stress that can lead to health-related problems and interpersonal relationship difficulties at work and at home. The first symptom so many of us notice is that we are not getting good-quality sleep. We go to bed tired and we wake up tired. It's no wonder that our performance at work can start to suffer.

The fact that you have taken the trouble to purchase and begin to read this book tells us that you may get stressed occasionally or are even suffering from chronic stress. Or perhaps you just want to learn more about stress management.

You have made a good decision! By the time you have worked through this book, you will understand more about the unhelpful thinking and self-defeating behaviour that can trigger stress. With hard work and practice, you will be able to tackle stressful events or too much pressure of work.

In addition to the main text, the book contains two key features. **Insight boxes**, just like the one below, relate to the section you are reading and provide key distillations of the topic in hand.

Insight
    We are largely responsible for how stressed we are.

Most importantly, each chapter provides useful **exercises** to assist you in understanding and tackling stress. Sometimes these will be relatively easy to undertake – a series of questionnaires, for example, will help you to assess your own particular stressors and just how well or badly you are dealing with them. Other exercises, however, will be more challenging, amounting to practical assignments for you to undertake, perhaps as part of your daily routine. We are aware that this may impose a heavy workload on you. Nonetheless, we believe that the benefits will make the effort worthwhile.

The exercises are the most important part of the book, and it is essential that you take them seriously. In reality, what you do and achieve is your choice.

As in our *Beat Low Self-Esteem with CBT* book (also part of the Teach Yourself series), there is some further 'bad news' about the exercises. They are not always 'one-offs'. Several of the points will be ongoing. This is because you will only internalize your new, more confident way of being by making your exercises your new default. In addition – something you will understand as you work on the tasks – we are looking for patterns that are personal to you, and this kind of detective work succeeds only when you have a good many samples to analyse.

The good news, though, is that – as we will emphasize in other parts of the book – nothing that we ask of you will take too long or be too difficult.

What is CBT in a nutshell?

The Cognitive Behavioural Therapy approach to coaching and therapy is based on how our thinking influences the way we feel and behaviourally react to situations. By using CBT techniques, we can modify our stress-inducing thinking in order to feel less stressed and act in more appropriate ways. For example, instead of feeling anxious about giving presentations to our colleagues at work and wanting to avoid the situation, by modifying our thinking we may only feel *concerned* about giving the presentation and may even look forward to the event. CBT is an evidence-based approach underpinned by numerous research papers highlighting its effectiveness.

How to use this book

First, you need some tools.

Do ensure that, before you start, you have purchased a notebook – preferably **a hard-covered A4 lined pad** – and that you have **a safe, personal place** to keep it. We ask you to use *hard-covered* pads as this will definitely give more cohesiveness to the stress-management work you are about to undertake. Of course, some readers may prefer to keep notes on their computer or mobile phone instead, as this may be more convenient and immediately accessible. However, if you are noting down personal experiences, thoughts and feelings on your computer, do keep them secure and preferably password-protected.

Once you have your tools to hand, take a look at the layout of this book. It is divided into ten chapters with a short final section entitled 'Taking it further'. Each chapter deals with different aspects of stress and stress management. Some will be more relevant to your own life and ideas than others, so you may wish to focus on those aspects that seem most closely to reflect your own problems.

We promise you now:

▶ Understanding stress will be interesting.
▶ We will spell things out in a punchy, common-sense way that you will grasp speedily and easily.
▶ You will see excellent results *quickly*.
▶ You will become an expert on the skills you need to manage or prevent stress, and that these will hopefully last a lifetime.
▶ We will stay alongside you every step of the way.
▶ Life will be so much better by the end of all your hard work.

Let's go!

1

Understanding stress and its symptoms

In this chapter you will learn:
- *to understand what stress actually is – what causes it and how to identify it*
- *about good stress and bad stress*
- *the different levels of stress*
- *the dangers of ignoring stress.*

What is stress?

The more you know about your enemies, the easier it is to overcome them. In this case, the enemy is stress. We talk about it, read about it, struggle with it – but what is it exactly? It is certainly one of the most commonly used words in the English language.

Does anyone *not* think they are stressed? In this day and age, we tend to look askance at the person who tells us that they do not suffer from stress. How can this be? Are they not living their life in the full-tilt, head-on, quart-into-a-pint-pot way that we are programmed to believe is the true way to fulfilment and reward?

While we hope you will find this book really helpful in assisting you in understanding and tackling stress, there are many other ways you can learn about stress. Stress advice proliferates in:

- ▶ bookshops
- ▶ television chat shows
- ▶ magazine articles
- ▶ chemists' shops

- ▶ over the garden fence
- ▶ and, more and more commonly, in doctors' surgeries.

What is your view of stress? Get out a note-pad (ideally, a hard-covered notebook that you can dedicate to being your **Stress Journal**), or use your computer or other electronic system for keeping notes, and write down what being, or feeling, stressed means to you.

Now see if your suggestions match ours. One way in which we can see stress is as a reaction you experience when you feel that, on the one hand, you have too much to cope with, but, on the other hand, it has got to be done, or life as you know it falls apart.

Stress comes along when…
ability to cope = less than situations that must be coped with.

Palmer, Cooper and Thomas (2003) suggest that 'Stress occurs when perceived pressure exceeds perceived ability to cope.'

Insight
Keep in mind the importance of that word 'perceived'. (More on this later.)

We also like the type of definition that you may already have taped up on your office wall, and which can be purchased on postcards in high-street shops (and of which there are many variations, we know), which goes along the lines of:

'Stress is created when your mind overrides the body's natural desire to choke the living daylights out of an idiot who is driving you completely crazy.'

However, stress can also be created by events outside our control, but to which we give a personal meaning that is at best negative, at worst catastrophic – that is, it is not our inability to cope that stresses us, but our lack of control over the situation.

Insight
Stress tends to occur when the 'to do' pile exceeds our perceived coping skills.

Exercise
Look back at any stressful situations in the last week. Jot them down if you have the time. (Shorthand will do.) Now write next to each one either 'WC' (within my control) or 'OC' (outside my control).

But I really can't control the stress in my life...

Well, actually you can!

When we asked for your definition(s) of stress, did you find that your own definitions were not too different to ours? What this means is that you actually know quite a lot about stress already.

The key points in managing stress are:

▶ *understanding* that you have to take responsibility for the stress in your life
▶ *applying* what you learn as you work through this book
▶ *believing* that if you do these things, you will be able to manage and even eliminate stress from your life.

These points are vital to take on board because the most important element in relieving stress is simply increasing your awareness of how you react to certain situations.

Insight
For the majority of us, the harsh truth is that a great amount of the inappropriate, unhealthy stress we encounter is self-induced.

We can almost hear you becoming quite indignant about this particular insight, but think for a moment: if that weren't true, there would be little point in us writing this book, and we would just have to accept that there is nothing we can do about stress.

The fact that reducing your stress levels is within your control is a bonus.

We are, of course, not talking about life's genuine traumas, which are far outside the remit of this book. Here, we are considering, and intending to help you with, the common-or-garden stress that seems to blight our lives daily both at home and at work and which comes from what appears to be the world in general (and possibly the boss in particular) giving you grief.

Exercise

Think of the most recent situation in which you felt really stressed. Write down what this was about and what happened. Now write down what you believe to be the cause of your stress in relation to that incident. Was it due to something outside your control? Or was there perhaps an element in your thinking that said, 'I can't cope with this'?

(Our goal at this point is just to begin to nudge you into the idea that you may have more control over what is going on than you have previously thought.)

Stress profiles

We all have our own personal **stress profiles.** You may notice this most commonly at work or in family situations. Something that really causes you stress has little effect on your partner or colleague (and that made you even more stressed, of course).

So you will need to focus in on and identify specific stress triggers that are personal to you and not worry too much about the fact that others don't worry about the same things that you do.

We want you to develop a stress profile that is specific to you.

This is exceedingly important as you are going to take responsibility for working on the issues that have the most effect in your particular life. There is no point in us giving you advice on overcoming the type of issues that stress us out if these may be things that scarcely cause your breath to quicken.

Learning to identify your own stress triggers is a very important skill.

Stress can be either…

▶ *chronic* (like a nagging toothache that we intend to find time to deal with, but almost learn to live with meanwhile), *or*

► *acute* (when we have such a severe bodily reaction to something that our coping mechanisms pack up immediately).

Stress hangs around in both these forms much of the time, and you need to start identifying what precipitates a stress reaction for you.

Exercise
Begin to keep a regular Stress Journal. As you gather more entries, you will start to see a pattern of the particular things that leave you feeling extremely stressed out. For the moment all we want you to log are stress triggers and stress outcomes.

To begin with, let's help you identify **stress triggers** alone. Simply draw a line down the centre of a page of your notebook and record a few events when you felt stressed, and what you think it was that caused the stress (Table 1.1). Remember, stress triggers are usually the things that push you over the edge when you were struggling to hang on by your fingertips in any event.

It should look like this:

Table 1.1   Simple stress trigger record

Event	Stress trigger
Piles of work on desk	Boss asked me when it would all be done
Rushing to leave work on time to see football on TV	Wife calls and asks me to collect daughter from friend's house

As you fill in the columns, you will begin to see just what makes you feel you have simply lost the plot. Notice whether these are major events or minor irritations. This will also help you recognize how stressed you are.

Insight
► We all have personal stress profiles.
► This explains why we can get upset by something that doesn't bother a friend at all.
► Learning about your own profile is key to dealing with your stress.

How much does stress affect you?

If you are still with us, then we are obviously all agreed that stress does affect you. The question is – how much?

A simple way to work this out is simply to rate it.

So next, we want you to start becoming familiar with the idea of rating your stress. Whether your stress is appropriate or not often depends less on the situation itself, and more on how stressful you personally perceive it to be.

For example, if you are waiting on a street corner for a friend who fails to appear, of course that will be extremely frustrating. Just how frustrating it seems will be dependent on many factors, including your own personal tolerance levels. Again, we'll go into lots more detail about this later, but for the moment we want you to start giving a **Personal Subjective Rating** (PSR) to your stress levels, which is also going to be a great tool for predicting patterns.

Use a 1–10 scale (if you are more comfortable with percentages, then 1–100 per cent is equally fine). Let's say PSR1 = scarcely bothered at all while PSR10 = incandescent with frustration.

Take heed of the P for 'personal' and S for 'subjective'. This is not higher maths – it is simply about how you feel at the time in your own words (numbers) – so go with your immediate gut reaction and record it.

Table 1.2 is a suggested layout for a PSR chart for your Stress Journal, though do feel free to adapt it if you prefer a different layout. We list a few examples to start you off.

A couple of points first… We will be working in more detail about the specific emotions engendered by stressful situations later on. For the moment, don't elaborate overly, just choose one of the following:

anxious, annoyed, upset, distressed, angry, worried. These will quite adequately describe your stress in most situations. (We are just looking for patterns at present, not detail.)

Secondly, we will be adding more detail to this journal in later chapters, so, for the moment, stick with it as a simple tool while you get used to stress awareness and rating its severity.

NOW FILL IN YOUR OWN EXAMPLES OF STRESS IN YOUR JOURNAL.

Table 1.2   Rating your stress

What happened? (my stress trigger)	When? (date and time)	How did I feel? (my stress outcome)	PSR (rate how I felt)
Locked self out of house	8.30 p.m. Monday	Furious, anxious	8
Train to work ½ hr late	7.45 a.m. Tuesday	Annoyed, frustrated	6
New work project dumped on me – impossible deadline	12.15 p.m. Wednesday	Worried, anxious	7

Keep this diary for two weeks at least – until you begin to notice patterns. Look out for the following:

▶ Do you get more stressed at certain times of the day?
▶ Do certain people seem to make you feel more stressed?
▶ Do stressful situations arise more in your workplace, home or social situations?
▶ Are there any particular connections that you can make? For example: 'I get more annoyed by events after a couple of drinks.'

Exercise

Get your diary and pen, and start your Stress Journal. One item per day will be enough – but you can write down as many as you wish.

What patterns, if any, are you noticing? Write them down.

Is stress always bad for you?

We tend to have a common view that all stress is a bad thing. This idea causes us to worry about it even more, as we absolutely don't want 'bad' things in our lives, and we set about rectifying the situation.

But hold on a moment – we often hear people say:

▶ 'I thrive on stress.'
▶ 'Stress is what motivates me.'
▶ 'I do my best work when I am really stressed.'

Does this mean that stress can sometimes be a good thing?

Actually, it does. **Good stress** (sometimes known as eustress) – or more accurately 'pressure', as we'll be calling it from now on – is what motivates us to stretch ourselves mentally and physically. It is what ensures that we get up in the morning, achieve our goals during the day, do our best to win at tennis, ensure that our children are loved and safe. These challenges are necessary for us all, to ensure that we grow and develop both ourselves and others.

Bad stress (which we call 'distress'), on the other hand, makes us feel swamped and incapable: it leaves us feeling anxious and depressed and takes much of the joy from our lives. While pressure encourages us to achieve more, bad stress usually manages to get us to achieve less.

How do we know whether the personal stress that we feel is helping us or hindering us? Well...

Earlier in the chapter we looked at rating our stress levels. We now need to work out whether these rates show our stress to be appropriate or inappropriate to the situation. It is inappropriate stress that we are more concerned with and we want to ensure that you learn how to get rid of this.

So how do we work this out?

Write down – in your diary, ideally, but on this occasion, the back of an envelope will do – what you think decides whether stress is good for you or bad for you.

Once you have done that let's see whether your answer matches ours...

> In day-to-day stressful situations, it is how you *view* an event that largely determines whether it is placing you under pressure (which is good stress) or stress (which is bad for you). No single situation categorically leads to bad stress. It is your *perception* of the event that decides whether the stress is good or bad.

We'll be giving you lots of skills for ensuring that you turn bad stress into challenging pressure or no stress at all later in the book. For the moment, your goal is to understand the principles.

Insight
Pressure can be good for us and improve our motivation.

Exercise
Take a page in your diary and draw a line down the middle or make two columns in your word-processing file if you are using your computer. Reflect on the times you have felt really stressed over the last week or two. On the left of the page, jot down stressful situations that caused you to react positively. On the right-hand side, write down stressful situations to which you have reacted negatively.

What does the page look like?

What does this tell you about your reactions to stress? (Don't worry if it all looks a bit negative. We will show you how to turn it around.)

But I'm under more pressure than others...

Actually, that's not what makes the difference. It is quite normal for us to view our own situation as being 'harder', or 'different', in order to justify why we are more affected by stress than the next person.

So read the following case study, and then we'll look at this idea again…

Jim and Peter both worked for the same organization at the same level, although in different departments. On 'nodding' terms in the corridor, they did not really know each other. When a promotional opportunity came up, both being reasonably ambitious, they decided, independently, to apply for it. They were not alone. Being an interesting job with a much higher salary than the one they were on, seven people in total tried out for the job.

After two rounds of interviews, the successful candidate was announced. It was neither Jim nor Peter. Both felt frustration and disappointment, and went home to rethink their positions.

Jim felt despairing. The whole process of applying for the position, the interviews and tests, the humiliation of rejection, the idea that he was obviously a poor employee who would never move up the company, were so stressful to Jim that he felt totally exhausted and depressed and decided never to put himself through the experience again. Jim continued to work in the same department for the next seven years until he was finally made redundant three years ago.

Peter also felt dreadful. He had found the process just as stressful as Jim. However, when he thought about it further he realized that of course moving up such a good organization was not going to be that easy. He resolved to discover which skills deficits in his experience had prevented him from being promoted, and to see whether, through extra training or self-learning, he could do something about it. He also never wanted to go through such a stressful experience again, and decided that the answer was obviously to be better prepared next time.

Peter got his promotion next time around, is still working for the company, and was in fact the manager responsible for telling Jim that he was being made redundant three years ago…

I suspect that, if we were able to speak to Jim or Peter now, their views would be very different. Jim would no doubt say that the stress he experienced was a bad thing and had a negative effect on his life. Peter, however (we would guess), would say that the stress he experienced was a catalyst for change, as it showed him that he had to strive harder in order to achieve the success that he desired.

Insight
In every situation, we can *choose* how we react. Our reaction to a situation is more important than the situation itself.

Focus on the following:

▶ The difference between pressure and stress (in regular, day-to-day situations) lies in our perceptions of the meaning of events, not the events themselves.
▶ We can turn our stress into pressure without avoiding stressful events.

Exercise
Think back over the last month. Has there been a stressful situation where you – on reflection – reacted in a negative way? Jot it down. Now jot down how you might have reacted in a different way that would have changed the outcome to a more positive one. Read the previous case study again if you need to.

What is the cause of all the stress we see around us and feel ourselves?

In general terms, what do you think are the major causes of stress in our society today? Where do you think that your own stress especially comes from?

Perhaps you are not quite sure, or haven't really thought about it. 'Stressed out' is perhaps just something that you feel on an ongoing basis without stopping to look at its specific causes – your personal stressors.

In this section we will look at some of the most common causes of stress, and ask you to think carefully as to whether they apply to you.

MAJOR STRESSORS
Your first steps to banishing stress will be made much easier if you know what your key personal stressors are.

First, do you have worries in any of the following areas:

- ▶ your job?
- ▶ your relationship?
- ▶ your health?
- ▶ your finances?
- ▶ your family?
- ▶ your social life?
- ▶ losing a loved one?

We hope, of course, you haven't said 'yes' to every one of them, but, if you have, don't worry – you can still sort it all out. These are what we call 'major stressors' and inability to cope (or to believe you can cope) in any one of these areas will be enough to send your stress rating sky high. They are also **generic,** in that they are all-pervading and seem to be 'around' all the time in some cases. (In other words, life seems to suck generally, whichever way you turn.)

Before moving on, there is one other stressor in a category all of its own. This is the stress caused by our increased expectations of life in general. We are a living in an era where 'having it all' is a popular mantra. Accepting this belief can lead to the problem of the reality of our lives not matching our expectations of how our lives should be. The less overlap there is between expectations and reality, the more stressed we become in trying to bring the two closer together, or feel frustrated that we cannot.

Exercise
Check out what 'having it all' means to you. What do you want most out of life that you are either aspiring to achieve, or pedalling fast to ensure you maintain? Copy and fill out the following form in your diary:

Job [for example]
To maintain present situation, I must _____
My future aspirations are _____

Material possessions [say]
To keep what I have now, I must _____
My future aspirations are _____

Self-development [possibly]

What I am doing now (e.g. read all current bestsellers, go to the theatre more often, etc.)_____

What else I wish to do _____

Now continue, until you have **ten** different 'having it all' expectations.

Insight

We need to do more than accept being 'stressed out'. We must *identify* our personal stressors, starting with the major ones.

We need to look at whether 'having it all' is contributing to our stress.

Exercise

Look at your 'having it all' list. Now rate them in importance to you – 1 being the most important, 10 being the least important.

A good question to ask yourself when attempting to make these ratings is: 'How much will this really enhance my life?'

Could you possibly, already, get rid of, say, numbers 9 and 10 (or more?). If you can, do. If you find this hard, leave it for the moment, but we will be looking for some reductions here by the end of the book.

MID-RANGE AND LESSER STRESSORS

Underneath the major stressors are what we call 'mid-range stressors'. These consist of very specific events and might include the following:

▶ your house being burgled
▶ your partner dumping you
▶ a minor car accident
▶ catching the flu
▶ having to cancel a holiday owing to a work deadline.

You know the sort of problem. You will find it easy to add many personally stressful situations to this list. All are frustrating and disappointing, but – as we have mentioned earlier – all dependent for the degree of stress on:

▶ your own frustration level, *and*
▶ your view of the importance of the event.

At the bottom of the pile are what we call 'minor stressors'. Extraordinarily, these can be the ones we identify with most easily when we decide that we simply cannot cope any more.

When discussing with someone else how stressed you are, you are more likely to mention one of the following minor stressors (rather than any of the major ones mentioned above):

- ▶ the lateness of your train
- ▶ leaving your mobile phone at home (when you are at work, or vice versa)
- ▶ the length of the queue in the supermarket versus the number of open checkouts
- ▶ finding that the DVD recorder has malfunctioned while recording the programme you really wanted to watch
- ▶ the rudeness of shop assistants
- ▶ the amount of time you have to wait on the line for a call centre to answer
- ▶ the washing machine repair man failing to turn up when you have waited in specially.

Again, some of these irritants will ring bells with most of you. Why do you think they spring to mind more quickly than the more generic stressors?

It is 'the straw that breaks the camel's back' principle coupled with the 'recency' principle. You struggle but manage, struggle but manage – and then the train to work is cancelled. This seems to 'finish you off', and is the most recent stress trigger you remember, so this is the moment you end up becoming frazzled and fed up.

It is important to understand this, as when we are looking for sources of stress, we need to look beyond the 'quick-fire' stressors. For example, when you inform your partner / work colleague that the train being late made you feel so stressed out that you could have cried/punched the announcement board, you are not really telling it how it is. The chances are, looking at the mid-term stressors, it was perhaps the cancelled holiday and, from the generic stressors, your whole work situation that were the real root cause.

So work as a whole is what needs to be looked at and possibly restructured to reduce the stress.

Exercise

Think about what has stressed you out most in the last week. Which category of stress did this stressor belong to? Think about the real source of this stress – in the way we outlined in the section above. On reflection, is the source of your stress a more ongoing and generic problem than the stressor you picked on? What do you learn from this?

Is managing stress really necessary?

Managing stress can involve quite a lot of work initially, while your new 'mellow defaults' kick in. Perhaps when you took the stress test earlier, it didn't turn out that badly. Like going on a diet, we start off enthusiastically, but as we get hungrier and hungrier, our resolve weakens and we begin to tell ourselves that perhaps we are not so overweight after all.

This is the time for reinforcements. You need to consider the costs of stress to reinforce the benefits of reducing it.

We need to emphasize that, when we discuss many of the costs of stress, we are talking about severe, prolonged stress over a long period of time. We are not concerned with the odd quickened heartbeat when you have to give a presentation, or the creeping anxiety you feel when you don't get a response to a job application. We are talking about stress over a long period that you chose to ignore, or think you can do nothing about.

Are you aware of the costs of prolonged stress? Can you imagine what they might be? Copy Table 1.3 into your Stress Journal, then write down as many possible personal costs of stress that you can think of and also consider the impact they have had on your family, friends and colleagues, too.

Table 1.3   The cost of prolonged stress

Cost of stress upon me	Cost of stress upon others I know

How many costs did you come up with? More than you had imagined? Have you ever thought about this before?

Insight
The costs of prolonged stress are too great to ignore.

Exercise
During the day, be alert for other costs of stress you may have overlooked. Note them down in your Stress Journal. Read over both the costs at least three times to ensure that you are familiar with them and can bring them to mind easily.

Don't ignore stress: you do so at your peril

With your list in front of you, take a look at how it matches with our list (below). There will be some (very many, probably) that you had not thought of, but, equally, you may have thought of some others not on this list. Does the sheer number of negatives surprise you?

Here is our list:

Physical costs

▶ high blood pressure leading to:
  ▷ increased risk of heart attack
  ▷ exhaustion
▶ weakened immune system leading to:
  ▷ increased risk of illness

▶ while not proven, research is looking at links between stress and an increased risk of cancer

Psychological costs

▶ low mood, with vulnerability to:
  ▷ depression
  ▷ anxiety
  ▷ sexual difficulties
  ▷ impaired cognition (clear thinking)
  ▷ sleep difficulties

Social costs

▶ relationship difficulties
▶ loss of self-esteem
▶ work difficulties including increased absenteeism that could lead to lower productivity or even job loses
▶ weakening of social links due to tiredness

We want to make sure that you consider this in a positive way, so let us now look at the benefits of managing stress.

First (and without peeping at the list below), write down for yourself as many benefits as you can think of.

In a way, of course, this is quite easy. We suspect you have simply reversed the costs of stress to discover the benefits of managing it. However, we still intend to print them up boldly, so that they are 'writ large' for you, and we ask you to refer to them *regularly* – each time, in fact, that you put this book to one side and feel that the effort is too much. We hope this reminder will consistently get you back on track.

Exercise
Photocopy or otherwise reproduce the list below, and ensure that you place it where you can review it constantly.

Read through the benefits at least three times to ensure that you are familiar with them and can bring them to mind easily.

THE BENEFITS OF STRESS MANAGEMENT

PHYSICAL GOOD HEALTH, INCLUDING

A STRONG IMMUNE SYSTEM

LOWERING OF YOUR RISK OF ILLNESS

INCLUDING HEART PROBLEMS

PSYCHOLOGICAL WELLNESS INCLUDING

GOOD MOOD, ABILITY TO RELAX,

CLEARER THINKING AND BETTER MEMORY

HIGH SELF-ESTEEM

IMPROVED SOCIAL RELATIONSHIPS

IMPROVED WORKPLACE RELATIONSHIPS AND PRODUCTIVITY

KEEP IN MIND

1 Stress comes along when your ability to cope is less than the situations with which you need to cope.

2 Stress is often caused by our lack of control over a given situation.

3 The first step in relieving stress is identifying how you react to certain situations.

4 You will have your own personal stress profile – things that cause you stress may not disturb others you live or work with. This, of course, works in reverse.

5 Develop a self-rating system for your stress. This will enable you to note and predict patterns in your stress profile.

6 Stress is not always bad – good stress ('pressure') is what motivates us to stretch ourselves mentally and physically.

7 In every situation we can choose how to react. Our reaction to a situation is more important than the situation itself.

8 Minor stressors such as your train being late can often appear to be the cause of your stress. Usually, however, they are just the straw that breaks the camel's back and you need to look deeper for serious causes of your stress.

9 Don't ignore stress. Its costs include physical, psychological and social consequences that can all be very serious.

10 Feel confident that you can reduce stress. You don't have to live with it but you will need to identify and accept its presence before you can start to get rid of it.

2

Learning how to measure and monitor your stress levels

In this chapter you will learn:
- *to easily spot the physical signs of stress*
- *to become aware of the psychological and behavioural signs*
- *to measure your stress in an accurate way*
- *to understand the physiology of stress reactions and how your body helps you out when your brain goes on strike.*

Signs and symptoms – how do you know you are stressed?

Learning to recognize the signs and symptoms of stress is an important skill. If you can react quickly at the first signs of stress, you will be able to 'nip it in the bud' before it gets to a stage where it can seriously harm you or cause you to act in a destructive way.

What are you looking for?

Common signs and symptoms of stress fall into three categories:

1 the physical signs
2 the psychological signs
3 the behavioural signs.

Let's look at these more closely.

PHYSICAL SIGNS AND SYMPTOMS

Physical symptoms of stress range from minor, scarcely noticeable situations, such as feeling tired, to the most dramatic of all – a heart attack. The longer you have been labouring under stress, the greater the likelihood of a more major problem.

Think about what happens when you are overwhelmed by stress. How do you feel physically? We suspect that you will have no trouble picking out some of the many possible symptoms we list below. Tick those that sound familiar.

Do you ever suffer from...

- ▶ sleep difficulties?
- ▶ changes in your eating patterns (stuffing, starving)?
- ▶ going to the toilet every two minutes?
- ▶ loss of interest in sex?
- ▶ feeling exhausted (even though you only got up half an hour ago)?
- ▶ heart palpitations?
- ▶ headaches?
- ▶ muscular tension?

As you will now have realized, these are some of your **alert signals** and you need to start playing detective – which means asking yourself questions about why you are tired, have muscle tension and so on, rather than simply accepting them as a fact of life. In further sections of the book, we will teach you techniques to relieve or remove all of the above symptoms. Once you have learned these skills, you will be able to nip physical stress symptoms in the bud very quickly.

Insight

Never just 'accept' physical symptoms. Even if you get a clean bill of health at the doctor's, don't just ignore things – look for stress-related reasons why you might be feeling this way.

Exercise

Look back over the last two weeks and think about any physical problems you may have had that cannot be explained away – for example, a broken arm caused by a rugby tackle doesn't count, but being inexplicably exhausted by 7 p.m. each night might be worth 'playing detective' over. Write these unexplained symptoms down, think about a possible explanation and write that down as well. Stress might be the answer, as we will find out.

Hopefully, these thoughts will not have turned you into a hypochondriac, but rather will have given you greater awareness of how stress manifests itself.

PSYCHOLOGICAL AND BEHAVIOURAL SIGNS AND SYMPTOMS

Psychological and behavioural symptoms may be noticed by you, but often it is your friends, family or work colleagues who point them out to you. It is not until someone mentions your current moodiness, for example, that you become aware of it yourself. So, when assessing these symptoms, do take heed of what others have to say. In fact, it is worth asking others directly, if you are uncertain. 'Have I been unusually short-tempered recently?' should elicit a response of 'yes' or 'no', although possibly the answer that you don't want to hear is 'You're always that way. What's new?'! (Time for anger management classes.)

Insight

Listen to your friends. If they tell you that you are behaving like a bad-tempered grouch, don't think 'it's them' – it may be you, and it may be an important signal.

BEING A MOODY GROUCH

Have you noticed, or have your friends pointed out to you, any of the following:

- ▶ increased moodiness?
- ▶ a short(er) temper?
- ▶ constant anxiety or panic attacks?
- ▶ finding it hard to get up in the mornings?

which might also mean that you...

- ▶ frequently bunk off work
- ▶ make 'silly' mistakes owing to poor concentration
- ▶ feel – or tell colleagues/friends etc. – that you just can't cope
- ▶ find even the funniest jokes fail to amuse you
- ▶ prefer to stay home rather than join the party.

Neither of these lists is exclusive – that would take a book in itself – but what we are intending to do here is to give you a broad enough picture of what you need to be aware of in order to ACT on rather than ACCEPT or IGNORE your symptoms.

An important question : When you feel stressed, what symptoms alert you first? Do you feel it in your body, or in your mind? Take your Stress Journal and write down the symptoms that especially apply to you. These will become your **red alerts** – the signals that warn you that you need to do something positive as soon as you can.

....

Insight

▶ You get physical and psychological warnings that you are stressed that can help you resolve matters before the results become too serious.

▶ Identifying those that are personal to you is a powerful skill.

▶ The more familiar you become with your own particular stressors, the more quickly you will spot them and can act on them.

....

How comfortable do you now feel with identifying stress-related symptoms? You have written them down and you have read about them above. Now, can you pinpoint them mentally, quickly and easily? Do you also understand why this is such an important skill?

Take a stress test to monitor your progress

Before you go any further, you really do need to know just how stressed you are, and how it shows up in your life. While we appreciate that you would not be reading this book if you were not stressed, completing the test below will help you to achieve a more specific, objective rating for your stress overall.

The key reason for doing this test is to help notice patterns that are specific to you, and hopefully give you both information and reassurance. You might even find that you do not need to read any further as your stress levels are lower than you thought.

Remember, stress shows up in physical, psychological and behavioural ways, so we are going to get you to measure all of these now. We would like you to take some copies of the next page, as we would like you to take this test again on a monthly basis. What we hope you will see, of course, is a reduction in the number of your symptoms.

Psychological stress response

Over the past month I notice that I get (feel/suffer from)…

Angry ☐	Anxious, apprehensive, frightened ☐
Ashamed, embarrassed ☐	Depressed, feeling low ☐
Guilty ☐	Jealous ☐
Moody ☐	Low self-esteem ☐
Feeling out of control ☐	Suicidal ideas ☐
Feeling helpless ☐	Paranoid thinking ☐
Unable to concentrate ☐	Intrusive images, thoughts, day dreaming ☐

TOTAL SCORE:

Behavioural stress response

Over the past month I notice that I get (feel/suffer from)…

Passive or aggressive behaviour ☐	Compulsive or impulsive behaviour ☐
Irritability ☐	Checking rituals ☐
Increased alcohol consumption ☐	Increased caffeine consumption ☐
Comfort eating ☐	Increased time off from work ☐
Poor sleep ☐	Withdrawing or sulking ☐
Increasingly accident-prone ☐	Lack of interest in sex ☐
Showing anger (banging with fists, etc.) ☐	Speaking too much or too quickly ☐

TOTAL SCORE:

Physical stress response

Over the past month I notice that I get (feel/suffer from)…

Frequent colds or other infections ☐	Indigestion ☐
Palpitations, or loud heartbeat ☐	Diarrhoea ☐
Breathlessness ☐	Constipation ☐
Tightness in chest ☐	Skin allergies ☐
Feeling faint or fainting ☐	Excessive sweating or clamminess ☐
Migraines ☐	Tension headaches ☐
Vague 'aches and pains' ☐	Rapid weight change ☐
Backache ☐	Menstrual problems, cystitis ☐

TOTAL SCORE:

TOTAL SCORE FOR ALL THREE SECTIONS:

Source: Adapted from C. Cooper and S. Palmer
Conquer Your Stress (London: CIPD, 2000).

Now look at the areas you have ticked. Do you respond to stress by having symptoms or possible signs in one particular area (such as behavioural), or are your ticks spread evenly across the three key areas? Often we find that our coaching or therapy clients tend to have responses in one or two key areas. However, once our clients become more aware of these symptoms or signs, then they can use them as a 'stress barometer' that allows them to take the initiative and tackle stress as soon as they recognize what's happening to them.

Incidentally, if you are regularly experiencing more than five of the possible stress signs, then you may wish to speak to your medical practitioner who will be able to advise you on a course of action. If you have ticked ten or more, it is likely you are suffering from very high levels of stress. However, remember that this short test is just an educational guide to help you become aware of some of the possible symptoms of stress. Some of the signs (such as suicidal ideas or chest pains) are obviously more serious than others – you may need to seek urgent professional attention. If you ever need to see a psychologist, they will use questionnaires that help them to assess clinical anxiety and depression that also ask how often a person has experienced the symptoms.

How stress can make you sick

We have headlined some of the costs of stress, and many of them, as you will have noticed, were *physical*. Some were more serious than others. Not all would be actually caused by stress – but stress can definitely make these problems worse, and/or prolong them.

Pill-popping stress relief

Every week several million people take some form of medication for stress-related illness. It is just possible that you, the reader, are one of them. This is not especially surprising once we have already acknowledged the very wide range of physiological changes that stress is capable of eliciting within our bodies.

Add to this the psychological changes – depression and a range of anxiety disorders – and that is a lot of sickness.

Stress and exercise

We often talk with clients who are suffering from stress. Some of the first questions we ask focus on lifestyle – most especially the amount of exercise taken. We never fail to be surprised by the number of clients who tell us that they don't exercise at all – 'I'm too busy', 'I used to, but gave it up', 'The gym closed down.' In a sense, they are telling us: 'I am much too stressed-out to think about exercise.' Yet exercise might just be their life-saver.

We take exercise seriously enough to devote a whole chapter of this book to it (Chapter 5). Please don't miss this – it is extremely important.

A simple question – and we will be asking this again later, so you might as well get ready now – how much exercise do you take at present?

In view of what you have learned above, are you prepared to do something more? Jot it down – we'll work harder on this with you in a later chapter.

How can I be sure that it's stress?

Think about any other 'irritations' you have had over the last months. Many of these may have been, or be, related to stress. Stress leads to muscular tension that can cause a variety of disorders – the stress headache being the most common. Chest pain, back pain, even grinding your teeth can all be symptoms of muscular reaction to stress.

Have you ever sat at dinner with someone when suddenly their stomach springs to life and they start to feel queasy and unwell? Often, when you solicitously ask what the problem is, the answer given is: 'I'm under so much stress – it's gone to my stomach. I think stress is giving me an ulcer.'

JUST AN EXCUSE?

However much of an excuse this sounds to cover up an embarrassing moment, it may well be partially true. A stressed stomach is probably the most common complaint after a stress headache. Your stomach lining becomes more acidic and can lead to a variety of gastric problems from simple diarrhoea to more intractable problems such as irritable bowel syndrome.

COULD IT BE AN ULCER?

Your friend is actually less likely to have a stress-induced ulcer, which is more likely to be caused by rogue bacteria. Nonetheless, stress can be the culprit, and all stomach complaints should be checked out for this.

IS IT DEFINITELY STRESS?

As therapists, doctors quite often send us patients with irritable bowel syndrome, which can successfully be sent on its way with stress-management techniques. However, in the last year one of the authors has twice worked with clients referred to her for stress, only to conclude early in their treatment that this was not the right diagnosis. In each case, a second medical opinion showed them to have a medical, not psychological, condition. So don't make any assumptions about the cause of your difficulties – check with your doctor first. If in real doubt, check with another doctor.

In the last 20 years or so there has been a growing amount of research undertaken to find links between stress and a variety of serious illnesses such as cancer, coronary heart disease, arthritis and so on. We need to point out, however, that at the time of writing, there is no conclusive evidence that these links exist. Equally, we would nonetheless like you to consider that such a link might be a possibility, and may perhaps be the strongest reason of all for learning how to control and/or eliminate stress for good.

Insight
While we regard stress as having, in the main, a psychological basis, there is no doubt that we can link it to a variety of physical illnesses.

However, ALWAYS ensure that you discuss any worries with your doctor before you make any assumptions in this regard.

Exercise
Make a written note of any aches and pains you have had recently, and then – considering what we have said in this section – write a big 'S' beside any that now sound as though they may have been caused by stress. (Does it make you feel better, or worse, to know that? It should make you feel better, as it will be a lot easier to get rid of stress than a pulmonary embolism, for example.)

Fight or flight – slay the stress dragon...

Our bodies have evolved to react to stress, and to help us out at times when our minds freeze or become befuddled. We need to understand something about how this has worked in our favour since time began, so that we can better appreciate how the fight-or-flight trigger can sometimes give us wrong signals and messages in the twenty-first century.

Feelings of stress are the result of a normal bodily reaction to danger or threat in the world about us. Scientists believe that it developed in the early days of primate evolution, when cave-dwellers faced many dangers in their lives. This bodily reaction, called 'autonomic arousal', helped prepare the caveman and cavewoman either to fight or run away when faced with danger. Cave dwelling in Neanderthal times was not a recipe for a long life. With a short lifespan, the

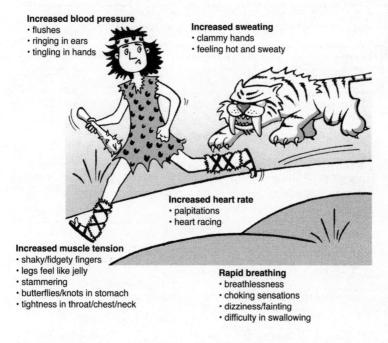

Increased blood pressure
- flushes
- ringing in ears
- tingling in hands

Increased sweating
- clammy hands
- feeling hot and sweaty

Increased heart rate
- palpitations
- heart racing

Increased muscle tension
- shaky/fidgety fingers
- legs feel like jelly
- stammering
- butterflies/knots in stomach
- tightness in throat/chest/neck

Rapid breathing
- breathlessness
- choking sensations
- dizziness/fainting
- difficulty in swallowing

Figure 2.1 Fight or flight – arousal responses inherited from prehistoric humans.

average stress trigger in those days would have been the roar of a sabre-toothed tiger or not being able to find sufficient food.

You can see from Figure 2.1 how this 'arousal' response causes many feelings and symptoms which are similar to those which occur when you feel stressed.

When facing danger, messages pass from the brain to different parts of the body telling it to speed up and be prepared for extra activity. This is your 'fight' or 'flight-or-fight' response. You will not be adversely affected physically in any way by these symptoms. Your body is simply responding to a 'danger' signal from the brain, and is trying to assist you to be ready to run or fight.

Exercise

Look back over the stress triggers you have written down. Put a star next to the stress trigger that provoked the greatest adverse physical reaction in the last seven days.

Were you concerned that you might be physically unwell, or did you need to sit down, recover, curtail any arrangements that you felt would be too draining in the circumstances? (Don't worry if you did – we'll look at this next.)

…Or run for your life?

Features of the age-old fight-or-flight response that you will recognize are:

▶ your heart beating faster (your brain has worked out that you may need more blood to be sent to your muscles for fleeing or fighting)
▶ you breathe more rapidly to increase the air supply to your lungs
▶ your liver releases extra glucose for quick energy
▶ your pupils dilate (to help you see the enemy – or the way to safety – more clearly).

In prehistoric times these physiological responses enabled us to deal as best as we could with the day-to-day stressors of that era – disease; threatening wild animals such as bears and hyenas; hostile groups competing for scarce resources, to name but a few.

However, what was helpful in prehistoric times can actually exacerbate our symptoms of stress in the modern era. If you understand this, it will no longer frighten you. The stresses we face today tend to be social or psychological – they are rarely life-threatening, and almost never require us to gear our bodies up for a major confrontation or to run like the wind from a dangerous situation.

Modern-day stresses might include pressure from the boss, missing a train, your car breaking down, losing your passport, 'one thing after another' going wrong – but you will not die from any of these situations. So, when that same old fight-or-flight response kicks in, it's overkill.

Your body has gone from reacting to over-reacting. You feel dreadful – some people even call their doctor, convinced they are seriously ill or about to have a heart attack. This is a bodily error message received from a stressed-out brain.

So first, do be assured that when you have these feelings, your body is simply trying to help you – you are physically fine! Second, we need to retrain our minds to stop producing these erroneous and physically exhausting error messages, and to 'get a grip'! We can achieve this both by adjusting our thinking, and using a variety of techniques to calm our bodies down. The next sections of this book will deal with exactly that.

Insight

▶ Fight or flight is a bodily response to help us survive physical danger.
▶ It serves us excellently when this is actually the case, but can cause us to receive 'error messages' about the scale of the problem.
▶ We can learn to correct these error messages, and, most importantly, even when we feel physically drained, no harm is being done to our bodies.

Exercise
Make sure that you understand the physiology of stress reactions so that you can be more aware of them when they arise. (Please look at Figure 2.1 again to remind yourself.) Think about what you will tell yourself next time you have worrying physical symptoms when you are feeling anxious or stressed.

Overcoming obstacles

Almost every time we make a decision to do something new or different – something that will give a result we feel we may get excited about – our enthusiasm for the project rises enormously. We hope that you are feeling this way about conquering your stress, especially now that your knowledge and understanding have improved hugely and we are about to embark on creating a toolbox of skills and techniques for you.

However, we are mindful that enthusiasm can wane! Remember those few pounds you vowed to lose that never actually came off? The oath to clear the clutter in the attic that, after you took one box-load to the dump, was soon forgotten? You get the gist. Projects we start with gusto can bite the dust if we don't find a lot of ways to prevent that happening.

So you need to develop some strategies to ensure that you are organized and prepared to countermand difficulties and excuses that may come up. You know yourself better than we can know you, so here is a question:

What are the most common excuses you give yourself permission to make when you want to bin something you wish you had not embarked on in the first place?

Please genuinely spend a moment or two thinking about this question. Write down your excuses.

Your answers will enable you to plan ahead of time with counter-suggestions to keep you going. For example:

- ▶ 'I'm just too busy and cannot find the time.'
  - ▷ 'I only need to find 15 minutes a day.'
  - ▷ 'I could find that at bedtime [for example].'
- ▶ 'I don't really feel so stressed now. Perhaps I don't need all this effort.'
  - ▷ 'I have suffered from stress for a long time.'
  - ▷ 'The fact that I am less stressed currently does not mean I have resolved my problems. In fact, it gives me more time and opportunity to learn these new skills for the future.'

- 'I've tried self-help books before and they don't seem to work.'
  - ▷ 'That does not mean this book won't work. It is action-oriented so, whatever happens, I am going to learn new skills and techniques on a daily basis.'

Insight

Don't fall at the first fence. Recognize your usual excuses and challenge them!

Exercise

Ask yourself honestly how often you bail out when things get difficult. What might make a difference? Would you need to give it more time? Would you need more self-belief? Do you simply take on more than you can properly commit to? Think about the most relevant excuse(s) to you (and then we will look in more detail at what you can do about them).

Tactics for knocking excuse-making on the head

We know that positive self-talk may not be enough when you really are too busy, aren't sure you need it, or come to a plateau in your learning. So here are some further suggestions.

GOAL SETTING

Make sure you have set yourself goals, but make these small and relatively easy to begin with. If you think in terms of 100 days, it may seem daunting. So think in terms of one day, or one week, and don't look beyond that.

SLOW DOWN

Alternatively, slow down. Decide to give yourself two days to complete a task instead of one, a week instead of a day. Take a complete break from time to time. Whatever one works for you. The important point with setting goals is that you are consistent about keeping to them. If they are too difficult, change them – but keep to whatever you have decided.

UNIQUENESS

We are all different. There may be parts of this book that seem less relevant to you personally, while other parts seem tailor-made for your personal lifestyle. So increase the time you spend on the areas that resonate with you and seem meaningful and helpful. Spend less time on the others. The only proviso we make is this: please at least look at all the sections – you just never know when something may strike a chord with you unexpectedly.

STICK WITH IT

We are always fascinated by the very quick results that clients hope for when working with us on personal psychological difficulties – stress management included! Yet, if we asked a client to go away and learn to play tennis to club team level, they would be unlikely to take two or three lessons and then give up because they had not already been selected for the club team. They would understand that it was all going to take a little longer than that. So be patient. You may have developed your stressful habits and lifestyle over a long period of time. While we *can* promise you major change in a reasonably short time, we cannot offer overnight success!

Revisit your goals – small successes will excite and encourage you. Reread your list of the benefits of managing stress to inspire you. Review the poor quality of your stressed-out lifestyle and look forward to how you would like it to be. Above all, we are here to do this with you – so don't you dare let us down!

Insight
▶ Be prepared. Set goals to suit you. Review them and change them so as not to pressurize yourself – but ensure that you stick to them.
▶ Be realistic – the fact that Rome was not built in a day did not prevent a beautiful city eventually being created.

Exercise
Take the time to write down how you plan to meet your goals for this course. Are your goals – 30 minutes per day, for example – realistic? Or would it be better to allocate less time and know that you would be more likely to stick to it? Are you able to work on this daily? Do you need to build in breaks? How will you handle extra pressures to ensure that you don't give up?

KEEP IN MIND...

▶ Reacting quickly to the first signs of stress is important if it is not to harm you or cause you to act in a destructive way.

▶ Stress often manifests itself in physical symptoms. These are your 'alert signals', so never simply accept them as a fact of life.

▶ Have your moods changed recently? Is your temper shorter or your anxiety greater? Stress can be the reason, so act on this information: don't just accept or ignore these changes.

▶ Stress can show up in physical, psychological and behavioural ways – be aware of them all.

▶ At its most serious, stress can be a significant factor in heart disease, so never ignore the symptoms.

▶ Don't rely on medication to reduce stress – you really need to be looking at lifestyle changes.

▶ Feelings of stress are the result of a normal bodily reaction to danger or threat in the world about us – they are actually our body's way of helping us to 'gear up' for fight or flight, rather than simply trying to make us sick.

▶ We need to retrain our minds to stop producing these erroneous and physically exhausting error messages. We can achieve this by learning to adjust our thinking and using a variety of techniques to calm our bodies down.

▶ Making changes is both hard and time-consuming and it can be easy to find excuses to let things slide. It is therefore important to develop some strategies to keep you on track – this will be the subject of the next chapters of this book.

▶ Make sure that the goals you set for yourself are realistic and give yourself more than adequate space and time to achieve them. Don't set yourself up to fail but, rather, make initial successes fairly easy to achieve and then build on that.

3

....

Thinking your way out of stress

In this chapter you will learn:
- *that thinking changes can help to reduce stress more easily than lifestyle changes*
- *the difference between facts and beliefs, and why this is so important*
- *how to begin to think more flexibly – and thus, less stressfully*
- *how negative beliefs can promote stressful consequences.*

Stress triggers

You now already know a great deal about stress and, especially, your own particular stressors – what presses your own personal buttons and makes you want to tear your hair out or strangle someone. You should also have some idea of the levels of stress that you are attempting to cope with, as well as seeing patterns of stress – what makes you feel better, what makes you feel worse...

Hopefully, you have also learned that stress can be reduced or eliminated, and that you won't necessarily have to change your life and move to a tree house in a mountain retreat in Tibet in order to find inner calm and a better-balanced life.

Now that you know all this, the real work starts. We are going to begin to help you to create a metaphorical **toolbox of de-stressing skills and techniques** that will ensure you are always in control of the situation.

You have learned the differences between pressure (which is good for you) and stress (which is bad for you). You will now be able to choose whether to run with pressure or eliminate stress.

One of the major ideas we put forward earlier is that it is not necessarily the *events* in our lives that cause stress (we know you will want to debate this proposition with us, but first bear with us to the end of this section), but rather:

▶ your *perceptions* of those events ('This is a catastrophe' versus 'It's not really that bad')
▶ your *default thinking style* (Are you a glass-half-empty person or a glass-half-full person?)
▶ your *attitudes* ('Shop assistants don't care about their customers' versus 'People are generally helpful').

The great news is that working on changing our thinking can be a lot easier than making drastic changes in our lifestyles. So we should give this a go first and see how far it works in relieving our stress. In the following chapters we will show you how to do this.

Insight
How you feel is more dependent on how you think about what happens than on what actually happens!

Exercise
Based on the above, what would you say is your default thinking style?

Stress responses

The American psychologist Dr Albert Ellis achieved fame in the 1960s for his innovative work in the area of thoughts and perceptions. He developed his model (Rational Emotive Behaviour Therapy) from the work of Eastern philosophers. Many of you will be familiar with Epictetus' famous pronouncement:

'People are disturbed not by things, but by the views that they take of them.'

We call this the **ABC model of stress,** and in this chapter we are going to give you the gist of the model. In the next chapters we will tell you how to use it to de-stress.

Think about this for a moment…

A = The Activating event or situation

For example, your boss hauls you over the coals for a poor piece of work.

C = Consequences

You feel depressed (emotional reaction), your stomach churns (physiological reaction), you have worrying thoughts about losing your job (psychological reaction), as a result of which you drown your sorrows in the pub (behavioural reaction).

Now here is a question:

Does it make sense to you that the Cs (the consequences) were caused by A (the event?)

Here is another question:

If you answered 'no', tell us why.

First, congratulations. If you ticked 'no', you were right. Now let's see if our explanation matches your own reasoning.

Above, we have referred to the ABC model. This is the crucial part…

It is the B that is responsible for the C, not the A.

B = Beliefs (about the event)

Your boss criticizing you was not responsible for any of the Consequences of this Activating event. Your Beliefs about the event were the cause. Your beliefs were your psychological reaction, which might have been 'I'll get the sack for this', 'I'm hopeless at my job', 'It's all downhill from here' and so on.

In the next chapter, we will start to look at making the changes that will reduce the negative, stress-inducing reactions that make us so miserable.

Insight

▶ We can reduce stress more easily by changing our thinking about our lives than by actually changing our lives.

▶ Events, in themselves, are not the stressors – but our beliefs about those events can make us extremely stressed.

Understanding your As (the activating events)

Let's take a look at events. We often cannot change what happens to us – our lives have many immovable elements and responsibilities – but all the same we need to learn how to deal with these events in a less stressful way.

What we mean by this is removing stressors. Where we can we should. So take a moment to think about the ways in which you may already do this.

AVOIDANCE

It doesn't make sense to put yourself into situations that you know are going to tense you right up and stress you right out. If I'm frightened of dogs, I can steer clear of dogs. If I don't like heights, the Eiffel Tower is not for me. If I'm not good a last-minute rushes, I can start my projects earlier on.

However, one weakness of avoidance is that it is often only a temporary quick-fix – a sort of plaster that you hope won't fall off. For example, if you loathe having to present at weekly team meetings, you may well be able to get out of it for a while, or pass it on to someone else. But, in the long run, you will be better off looking at why it bothers you so much and then learn to face your fear.

STOPPING

Often we 'go along' with difficult situations in a robotic way, until we hear ourselves (or someone else) say, 'Why am I / are you doing this?'

Why are you ironing hankies, bringing six other people a cup of coffee every time you get one, putting up with the guy who sits next to you at lunch each day droning on and on about his problems?

Stop doing it!

Do you get in to work each day and have to hit the coffee machine six times to get it to give you that 'kick-start' cuppa that you need? Start to think creatively – why not bring in a kettle and some coffee sachets? Why not call in at a coffee shop on the way into work?

We all know many people who constantly gripe and complain about their mobile phone that plays up, the uncomfortable chair that they sit in, the way their desk faces a poor outlook or that the lighting is not to their liking.

So change it!

Where you can add resources that will make your life, easier, calmer and less bothersome, just do it!

RETHINKING

Similar to avoidance, rethinking means being aware that you don't need to put up with a stressful situation, but that you use a certain amount of creative thinking instead of simply dodging the issue – 'Instead of doing something *this* way, could I perhaps do it *that* way?'

Insight

Four ways of changing your As and removing stressors are: avoidance, stopping, adding resources, and/or rethinking.

Exercise

Look back over the last week. Think of one example of avoidance, one where you could actually just 'stop it', one where you might change things, and one where you might rethink the situation.

Write these down with the date next to them.

In about a week's time, check which of these situations you have actually learned to react to differently.

Challenging your As

Think of half a dozen situations right now that you get stressed about on a day-to-day basis. Then stop and think for a moment about any changes that could make life easier.

We'll start you off…

Table 3.1 Making adjustments

Stressful event	Adjustment(s) I could make
Getting the children ready on time for school in the mornings is hugely stressful.	▶ We could all get up earlier. ▶ I could get up before the children. ▶ We could get stuff ready the previous evening. ▶ I can let others take more responsibility for ensuring that they're ready. If they're not, they're not. They'll learn!
The traffic on your way to work gets worse and worse. By the time you arrive now, you have smoke coming out of your ears from frustration.	▶ I could leave earlier and take the longer but less traffic-ridden route. ▶ I could look at public transport – at least I could read on the train. ▶ I could invest in some audiotapes of books I want to read and never have time. (That might be fun!)

These examples may be way off the mark for you, but they will give you the idea. Now write down some ideas of your own. Then brainstorm possible adjustments and think how this approach might work for you.

In this chapter, we are not talking about major life changes – that comes later. This is simply about getting you to look at everyday stressors that you could possibly make changes to now – but have not thought about yet.

Insight

Only change things that you get really stressed about. A lot of what goes on is more to do with your attitude – we'll look at that next.

But facts are facts... or are they really beliefs?

It doesn't matter how strongly or fervently you believe something – that doesn't necessarily make it true. One of the difficulties that many of us have is appreciating the difference between a belief and a fact. Here are some examples:

- ▶ I can't sew.
- ▶ Meat is bad for you.
- ▶ Driving at night is more dangerous than driving in the daytime.
- ▶ Home-made lasagne is better for you than shop-bought lasagne.
- ▶ Babies need to be fed four-hourly to ensure they develop a routine.

- ▶ The government is useless.
- ▶ Nobody cares about me.
- ▶ Flying is really dangerous.
- ▶ I could earn a lot more money working for XYZ Co.

How many of the above statements do you think are beliefs? And how many do you think are facts? How easy was it to tell the difference? We suspect you may not have found it as straightforward as you thought. We often tend – especially when under stress – to operate on the principle that a belief is a fact. This is problematic when we are trying to decide on the meaning of an event since, while beliefs can be challenged, facts are facts and, therefore, unchallengeable.

Now test out your own stress-inducing beliefs. The questionnaire below is taken from S. Palmer, 'The Negative Travel Beliefs Questionnaire (NTBQ)', *The Rational Behavioural Therapist* 7/1 (1999), pp. 48–51.

Questionnaire: Beliefs indicator test

Do you recognize any of the following? The questions include both work and general beliefs. Circle, or write down, the strength of your belief, where S represents 'strongly', M represents 'moderately' and W represents 'weakly'. Include in Question 25 any additional beliefs you hold that cause you further stress.

1	S	M	W	Events should go smoothly.
2	S	M	W	Work must be exciting and stimulating.
3	S	M	W	If I lost my job, it would be awful.

4	S	M	W	If I lost my job, I could not bear it.
5	S	M	W	My job is one of the most important things to me.
6	S	M	W	I must perform well at all important tasks.
7	S	M	W	My work should be recognized by others.
8	S	M	W	I am indispensable at work.
9	S	M	W	I must enjoy myself whatever I am doing.
10	S	M	W	I must not get bored.
11	S	M	W	I should not encounter problems.
12	S	M	W	I should have the solitude I deserve.
13	S	M	W	I must escape from responsibilities and demands.
14	S	M	W	I should be treated fairly.
15	S	M	W	I should be treated as special.
16	S	M	W	I should be in control of all significant situations.
17	S	M	W	Others should respect me.
18	S	M	W	I should get on well with my friends and family.
19	S	M	W	My children should do well in life.
20	S	M	W	If things went badly, it would be awful.
21	S	M	W	If things went badly, I could not stand it.
22	S	M	W	Things never work out well for me.
23	S	M	W	If things go wrong, those responsible are stupid, useless, idiots or failures.
24	S	M	W	If I fail at a task, that proves I'm a failure or useless.
25	S	M	W	Additional beliefs:

....

Now, count up how many Ss you found. What does this tell you?

You know the answer, of course – the beliefs you hold (which ARE subjective, by the way!) are a major cause of your stress. Next we'll take a look at what you can do about this problem.

....

Insight
- ▶ It is not always as easy as we think to tell the difference between a belief and a fact.
- ▶ We need to learn to tell the difference if we are to reduce stress-induced thinking.
....

But why should I change my beliefs?

Well, you certainly don't have to, but, if you are reading this book, you will by now have realized that some of your beliefs may be stress-inducing and self-defeating. So it makes sense to adjust those that are not helping you. Many of your beliefs will be beneficial – we are looking only at those that cause you stress.

So how do you make a change? It's quite simple really.

> Remember, beliefs are NOT necessarily facts. They are thoughts that you may have had for a while, based on certain *assumptions* (we'll talk more about assumptions later) but they really are open to question and debate.

Who will you debate them with?

Yourself, of course!

Let's get you started.

Look again at the beliefs indicator test you have just done.

First of all, get a pen and strike through each of the following words each time it appears:

SHOULD   MUST   NEVER   STAND   BEAR   AWFUL

This leaves a lot of gaps, doesn't it?

LEARNING TO BE LESS RIGID IN YOUR THINKING

Now you need to replace each of these words with a 'softer' word, phrase or sentence. For example, instead of 'Events should go smoothly' replace this with (for example) 'It would be nice if events always went smoothly'. Work through the rest of the gaps, making similar replacements.

Next, start challenging some of these beliefs. You will need to write these down. We are going to be asking you to start challenging many thoughts and beliefs that you have on a regular basis, so this is to get you into the habit. We'll refer to this idea quite often now, until you begin to internalize it.

Pick six of the beliefs listed that you feel apply to you. For example:

> ## Belief: 'I should be treated fairly.'
>
> Really? Why?
> ▶ Realistic alternatives:
>   ▷ 'While it is great to be treated fairly, realistically we sometimes get a bum deal.'
>   ▷ 'I probably get treated fairly more often than not.'
>   ▷ 'Everyone has their own idea of what fair treatment is.'

Work on some more. On each occasion, come up with at least two or three alternatives. You don't have to totally believe them yet. We are just teaching you to stretch your thinking.

Insight
Beliefs are not facts, and can be wrong.

By ridding our thinking of 'extreme' wording, and replacing it with 'softer' wording, we actually disturb ourselves less.

Challenging stress-inducing beliefs can help us to see situations and events in a more relaxed way.

Exercise
Write down some challenges to the six beliefs that you noted down earlier. Don't worry if you don't actually 'believe' them. This is just to help you learn to think more broadly and flexibly. Two or three alternatives can be your goal.

How Bs (beliefs) affect Cs (consequences)

James plays football on Sunday mornings. Every Sunday at 9 a.m. sharp, he gets the bus to the football ground to join his mates for a friendly game. They usually play another local team, and occasionally they play in league games.

One weekend, James had a big night out on the Saturday evening. He also forgot to set his alarm clock. He woke up on Sunday morning at 9.15 a.m. James leapt out of bed in shock, and then he thought, 'This is hopeless. I'll never get there in time now. Everyone will be so cross. In fact, I'll probably get dropped from the team, since I haven't been playing that well recently. They'll ask Rob instead now.' As James thought these ideas, he began to feel really upset. Depressed, he lay back on the bed and resolved that he might even resign from the team before he got pushed. He closed his eyes and fell back to sleep.

Later in the day, the phone rang. It was one of his team-mates. 'Hi, James – where did you get to this morning?' James sighed. 'Oh, I overslept. It was just all too late – I knew Rob would replace me. I expect he played really well?' 'You idiot, James!' came the reply. 'You should just have come along in any event. Three members of the opposition failed to turn up, and one of our lot got badly injured in the first five minutes, so the whole game was held up until 11 a.m., and we really missed you.'

You will know what we are going to ask you now, and you will have your answers at the ready.

> *Did James miss a great game of football because of his 'A' (getting up late) or because of his 'B' (his beliefs about how awful this was)?*

What were the consequences to James of this? Well, there were several...

▶ he felt really upset
▶ he went back to sleep
▶ he missed a great game of football.

So the moral is: if you want to change your Cs and you can't change your As, you need to change your Bs.

We have now looked at As, Bs and Cs on their own. Now we are going to bring the whole thing together, and throw in Ds and Es (no more alphabet letters after this, we promise).

Insight
- ▶ A–C thinking allows us to blame external events or other people for our stress, which is hard to address as we have little control over the situation.
- ▶ B–C thinking helps us to take responsibility for our stress – which is good news as it means we can work on changing things.

Exercise
Read through James's story again. Jot down some alternative Bs that he might have had that would have changed the consequences of that day for him. Attempt to come up with at least two or three alternatives.

Ds and Es – what are they?

D = Disputing belief

E = Energizing outcome

While an energizing outcome cannot always be the answer to all your prayers, it will – exactly as the name implies – make things a great deal better than the negative consequences of the negative belief.

CHART IT

Table 3.2 – the A–E chart – explains this clearly. We have given you a simple example (we do appreciate that this may be nothing like the stresses you have, but it gives you the jist) and we would like you to copy this into your Stress Journal and fill in two or three other stressful situations (either ongoing, or 'one-offs'). Follow through with the beliefs and consequences – and then add your D and E.

WRITE IT DOWN

Many people say, 'Oh, I don't need to write that down – I can just think it though in my head.' Or you might write it down just occasionally. Or never.

Table 3.2 Sample thought record – challenging your negative beliefs

A ADVERSITY	B NEGATIVE BELIEF	C NEGATIVE CONSEQUENCE(S)	D DISPUTING BELIEF	E ENERGIZING OUTCOME
Turned down for job interview several times	'I'm not good enough.' 'I'll never get a job.'	Feel depressed Lose confidence Stop bothering	'Jobs are hard to come by for everyone, it's not personal – I'll have another go as I do have lots to offer.'	Have another go at getting an interview. Increases confidence, eventually will get job offer.

It really helps to write it down.

Writing your thoughts down will make you think harder, and for longer, and will train your brain far better to make changing thought patterns more automatic. Once that happens, then you can stop writing as your brain will automatically look at things differently.

We will talk in more detail about 'thought challenging' later.

Insight

Ds and Es are an important part of your total thinking processes.

They are important because they help you to dispute your initial thinking, and this will, hopefully, give you a better outcome.

Exercise

Use the A–E chart to practise challenging some of the beliefs that cause you to feel particularly stressed. (Examples might be, 'There is rarely enough time to do what I want', 'I often feel like a victim of outside circumstances', 'I should always be very generous and unselfish'.)

BUT IT'S NOT THAT EASY!

From what we have done so far, you can see that the way you think has an important effect on the way you feel and what you are able to do. Pessimistic, negative thoughts such as 'I can't cope' or 'I feel terrible' make you feel more anxious and unhappy and can themselves be a major cause of your stress.

This is negative B–C thinking, and you are now learning to dispute and challenge these thoughts and beliefs.

However, it is one thing to understand all this in theory, but quite another to be able to easily make the necessary changes. Clients often tell us, 'They are always there. I don't know where they come from and cannot do anything about them.' This is one of the major problems people find in getting rid of stressful, depressive thoughts and ruminations. They seem to invade our brains and we just don't know where they came from. Sometimes they are called 'pop-up' thoughts.

Be aware of negative thoughts

Just becoming aware of these negative thoughts can help you to understand why you are worried by them, and is the initial step towards reducing negative emotions, and learning to think in a more helpful, constructive way. To help you become more aware of these thoughts, you need to know a little more about what negative thoughts 'look like'. The list below suggests characteristics that these thoughts have in common:

▶ They spring to mind without any effort from you.
▶ They are easy to believe.
▶ They are often not true.
▶ They can be difficult to stop.
▶ They are unhelpful.
▶ They keep you anxious and make it difficult to change.

These negative thoughts may be difficult to spot to start with – you are probably not always aware that you have them – and the first step is to learn to recognize them. This is where some of the previous work we have done now comes in. We have started helping you to challenge beliefs where you may not previously have considered any alternatives. You have done an exercise where you start to consider new Ds.

You may remember how earlier we said, 'It doesn't matter if you don't believe them yet', and this is really true. What you are doing is learning to think more broadly, and often more optimistically, too, and in time your 'negative automatic thoughts' will stop being the first ideas that come into your head. More hopeful and helpful thinking will become the norm.

Insight
▶ We understand that changing your thinking is not always that easy, but we promise you that learning to identify your thinking errors is a first, good step.
▶ Once you have achieved this, you will find it easier to replace negative thoughts with more helpful ones.

Exercise
Cover up the section in this chapter that suggests some characteristics of negative automatic thoughts. Now write down how many of the characteristics you can remember.

This exercise is important in helping you to begin to recognize faulty thinking patterns more easily.

I'm challenging Bs – but what do I replace them with?

You should by now have a better idea of how answering your negative thoughts in a more helpful, realistic way can help you to cope with your worries. However, it can still be hard to think of coping thoughts or statements (your Ds) that will help you answer your own particular negative thoughts.

To help you do this, here is a list of coping statements which may give you some ideas. Read through the following list and think about which of these might apply to you and help you to deal with your worries in a more positive and constructive way:

Coping statements

- ▶ I'm going to face this problem/situation so that I can practise coping better.
- ▶ It's unlikely that it will work completely, but the important issue is to practise and build up my confidence.
- ▶ I know that worry makes me feel worse. I know my feelings can be controlled.
- ▶ I've been in this position before and have come out of it alive / still in one piece.
- ▶ I know I'll get better the more I get used to coping with stress.
- ▶ I'll feel so proud of myself when I feel myself getting calmer.
- ▶ It feels good learning how to control stressful feelings.
- ▶ I'm deliberately going to change how I feel.
- ▶ I'm living proof that I can stand almost everything.

The above are just examples to get you started. Now think up at least six coping statements of your own that are relevant to your particular problems.

The key to thinking in a more balanced way is to keep practising. Every time you become aware of negative thoughts going through you mind, stop yourself and think of a realistic and helpful alternative to it.

When preparing to go into a situation that you know will be extremely stressful, think beforehand about what coping skills you will use (e.g. perhaps a breathing exercise – see Chapter 5) and how you will answer any negative thoughts before, during and afterwards.

When you suspect that your thoughts are negative or unrealistic, ask yourself:

▶ Is this really true?
▶ Is there another way of looking at this?
▶ What was I afraid might be going to happen?
▶ What was happening, or in my mind, just before I began feeling this way?
▶ Am I recalling any past incidences where things turned out poorly?

Being prepared is half the battle of helping you to cope.

Insight
▶ Having a 'stock' of coping statements can help us deal better with stressful periods.
▶ Preparing ahead of time, when you know you are going into a stressful situation, can make a huge difference.

Exercise
Start your own list of coping statements. Write down at least a dozen straight away. Add to this list regularly and read them regularly.

A reminder... write it down!

One of the most important issues to keep up with is the form we gave you for challenging your negative beliefs (Table 3.2). This type of form is often called a **thought record**, because, although they are recording what has happened, the main focus is on what you *thought about* what happened.

The more you practise filling in a thought record, the easier it becomes to spot these thoughts, and to understand the effect they have on how you feel.

It may be quite a new idea, to remember what you were thinking when you were worried or feeling low, and may take some practice before you get the hang of it. Next time you find yourself becoming tense or worried, as soon as you can, sit down and fill in your thought record. You can describe the physical sensations you experienced as well as the thoughts that went through your head at the time.

Once you are familiar with identifying negative thoughts, you can keep track of them and examine how unrealistic or unhelpful they are and whether they are useful to you. As you learned previously, if they are unrealistic or unhelpful you can challenge them with what we call a disputing belief. You will now be becoming familiar with this – your D – the reply that you make to these thoughts, based on firm evidence. Studies have shown that doing this can improve your mood and make you feel more in control of your situation and your life.

Insight
▶ Simply having an awareness of negative thinking (rather than assuming that it is rational thinking!) can help us feel better.
▶ The more often you jot these thoughts down in your Stress Journal, the easier they will become to spot – and then dispute.

Exercise
Jot down – either using a thought record (Table 3.2) or just on the back of an envelope – two stressful thoughts you have had today. Would you call those thoughts negative thoughts or rational thoughts? Now keep going with increasing your awareness of your thinking when you are stressed.

KEEP IN MIND

▶ Make sure you understand the difference between *pressure* (which is good for you) and *stress* (which is bad for you).

▶ It is not necessarily the events in your life that cause you to be stressed but your *perception* of those events, your *default thinking style* and your *attitudes*.

▶ Understand the ABC model of stress, where A is the activating event, B is your belief about that event and C is the consequence(s) of your belief.

▶ A–C thinking allows you to blame external events for your stress, while B–C thinking helps you to take responsibility for your stress and effect real change.

▶ Appreciate the difference between belief and fact. You can believe something with your heart and soul – but that doesn't make it true. Develop a real awareness of this and become more open-minded.

▶ Beliefs are simply assumptions that are open to question and debate. Who is the best person to debate them with? Yourself, of course!

▶ Start to delete 'shoulds', 'musts' and 'oughts' from your vocabulary and replace them with 'softer' alternatives. This helps you to learn to be less rigid in your thinking.

▶ Start with simply becoming aware of your negative, pessimistic thinking. This is the initial step towards reducing negative emotions and learning to think in a more helpful, constructive way.

▶ Coping statements are helpful when you feel negative. Develop a list of them. The key is to keep practising – each time you become aware of negative or anxious thoughts, find a coping statement to counteract them.

▶ The best way of changing your thinking is to start by writing down your negative thoughts and then write down at least two or three coping statements. Writing things down gives them much more impact and ensures that your brain absorbs and develops this new way of thinking.

4

Become a detective – tracking down your stress

In this chapter you will learn:
- *how thinking errors can prevent thought challenging from reducing stress*
- *to better understand the role that emotions play in stressful situations*
- *to begin to identify thinking errors that can cause your stress to rise*
- *to 'play detective' to check out your thinking.*

Tracking down stress triggers

While challenging our negative thinking and beliefs is one of the most important tools in defeating stress, it is not always such a simple task as it sounds. We sometimes hear people saying, 'Oh, that's all very well, but it never works for me.' We are always curious about this! If it is not working, then there will be good reasons for that, which can be corrected.

One of the more obvious reasons many people find that 'thought challenging' has no helpful effect is that they are challenging the wrong thought.

In order to properly challenge our negative thoughts and beliefs, we need to be sure we are accurately working out just what the correct negative thought – the **stress trigger** – is.

For example, imagine you feel so stressed out that you need to sit down and breathe deeply in order to recover. Then you ask yourself what might have caused that, and the thought that comes into your mind is:

> *'I wasn't sure what to cook for dinner tonight.'*

Really? Not knowing what to cook for dinner tonight caused you to feel so stressed and upset that you had to sit down?

So you need to dig a little deeper to access what was really bothering you, in order to deal with the problem.

In this case, for instance, further probing may have uncovered that the reason you were so stressed is that your relationship had been on very shaky ground recently. Among other problems, your partner had been very critical of your cooking, and the previous evening there had been a big row over the fact that you should have known he didn't like sausages.

Now the stress levels make more sense, don't they?

Insight
When thought challenging doesn't seem to help lift your mood, you may be challenging the wrong thought.

Exercise
Have you felt stressed in the last week, without being able to pinpoint quite why?

Write down the times that you felt this way, where you were, and what you were doing. That's all for the moment. We will shortly suggest some skills to help you solve these mysteries.

Digging deeper – unearthing the real problem

One of the biggest problems for people who feel stressed out on a chronic, ongoing basis is that of pinpointing exactly what the problem is. Here are some skills that we would like you to use when 'digging around' to discover what thoughts or beliefs are really stressing you out:

RATE IT

This means rating your stress levels, on the one hand, as well as the importance of your thought, on the other, and seeing whether there is a 'match'.

For example, if your mood rating is 'Stress (90 per cent)', a negative thought on the lines of 'My friend has forgotten our lunch appointment' is not going to be the causal thought – that is, the real stress trigger that causes the emotion. If you rate the importance of that thought, it is probably going to be around 20–30 per cent.

So ask yourself, 'Why does that matter?' and you are more likely to get to the correct stress trigger – which in this case, could be, 'Perhaps she has been involved in a serious accident.'

This leads us to the Downward Arrow.

THE DOWNWARD ARROW

This is an excellent skill for getting to the bottom of your stresses! You can use it in a variety of situations – and with others as well as yourself. It works like this:

You feel dreadfully stressed and your head is aching. Why is this? Your first thought is:

> *'I can't seem to get on with the work I need to do for this presentation.'*

The first question is:
↓
'Why does that matter?'

The answer is:

> *'If the presentation doesn't go well, we may lose the client.'*

The second question is:
↓
'Why does that matter?'

The answer is:

> *'If we lose the client, our department won't meet its sales targets.'*

The third question is (you're getting it now, aren't you?):
↓
'Why does that matter?'

The answer is:

'I'll be held responsible and I may even lose my job.'

We won't go on further with 'Why does that matter?' as you will understand the principle now, but in theory, of course, you could ask yourself another question instead:

'What is the personal meaning to me if this does or doesn't occur?'

Exercise
Practise using the Downward Arrow with the stressful occasions you noted in the last exercise. See what you discover about the stress triggers that are REALLY bothering you.

Do our emotions cause stress, or does stress cause our emotions, or both?

We've spent some time looking at thoughts, and how they can affect us. Our reaction to stress, however, isn't just thoughts – it consists of feelings, too. It can sometimes seem a very physical feeling ('I'm so stressed I'm exhausted'), or sometimes it can seem to be a very emotional feeling ('I'm so stressed I could cry').

We learned earlier in this book how negative thinking can cause negative outcomes, and the emotional outcome can be quite powerful. So you can appreciate how negative beliefs can lead to negative emotions.

If Paul feels anxious about getting a poor work appraisal and has decided that this means he'll be first on the redundancy list, then the stress trigger is his negative belief (i.e. 'I'll be first on the redundancy list'). That, in turn, triggers his feelings of anxiety that cause him to get quite stressed out about the situation.

The negative appraisal of the situation is what is making Paul feel anxious.

Equally, however, negative emotions can trigger negative beliefs that trigger further negative emotions.

Jenny was asked, at the end of an already long, hard day, to work late in order to finish an important project within an unreasonably short time frame. She started feeling very anxious about reaching the deadline. Then she became aware of her physical symptoms of anxiety such as her heart beating rapidly. She started to wonder 'Am I OK? Am I seriously ill?' She literally became anxious about her anxiety! Feeling so stressed out, Jenny found it hard to focus on her work.

The negative emotion of anxiety associated with meeting deadlines triggered physical symptoms (such as a rapid heartbeat) that Jenny then had worrying, pessimistic thoughts about – triggering more anxiety.

As we found in the first section of this book, stress can be caused by a variety of different moods or emotions, and it is important to learn how to identify these. For example, you might feel tired all the time, but fail to realize that this is because you are depressed.

So recognizing moods and understanding how they can affect our thinking, just as much as our thinking can affect our moods, is another important aspect of learning to conquer stress. In the next section, we'll help you to more easily identify your moods…

Insight
- ▶ Our emotions drive our thinking just as powerfully as our thinking drives our emotions.
- ▶ It is therefore very important for us to be able to *identify* our emotions.

Exercise
Can you think of an example, in the past week or two, when you have allowed negative emotions to turn into negative thinking? Jot it down.

Now find an example of negative thinking that led to a negative emotion. Jot that down as well.

What do you learn from this?

Identifying stressful emotions

We have already seen how thought can sometimes be difficult to identify specifically. This can apply to emotions as well, so here are some suggestions to help you to identify a variety of moods that you might feel in a day:

Moods

anxious	scared	shy	panicky	insecure
sad	hurt	depressed	disappointed	empty
angry	irritated	frustrated	appalled	embarrassed
humiliated	repulsed	sick	nauseous	guilty
ashamed	jealous	envious	shocked	surprised
happy	excited	content	proud	concerned

Now do two small exercises…

1 Write down any further suggestions you have to add to this list and then…

2 Take a highlighter pen and score through which of the above moods you have been most aware of in the past month.

Note: if you have a problem identifying emotions, then being aware of bodily changes will often help you – stomach churning or palpitations can signal acute anxiety or panic, while heaviness throughout your body can signal depression, for example.

Copy Table 4.1 into your Stress Journal and use it to write down the three negative emotions that have cropped up most frequently and what the situation was when you felt these emotions. Can you recall what you were thinking on any of the occasions that these moods cropped up?

An important point here is that there should be a 'match' between the intensity of the thought and the intensity of the emotion. We have worked on this already (see 'Rate it' section earlier in this chapter), but make it a default to check this out. If there is no match, use some of the skills you have learned to ensure that you get one.

Table 4.1   Connecting thoughts and feelings

	What was the situation?	What was I thinking?	Negative emotion
1			
2			
3			

You will hopefully now have an increased ability to recognize emotions that may be causing stress, as we are more understanding of how negative thoughts can cause negative emotions.

All this boils down to the same principle:

If we can replace our negative, unhelpful thoughts and beliefs with more constructive ones, we will also feel a great deal better emotionally:

THOUGHTS drive EMOTIONS and EMOTIONS drive THINKING.

Insight
▶ Really absorb the statement above connecting thoughts and emotions and you will become much more able to control how you feel.
▶ Practise being aware of your emotions as well as your thoughts. If there is a 'mismatch', you are not addressing the problem.

Exercise
Make sure that the thoughts and feelings box (Table 4.1) we have asked you to fill in has been done.

Continue to have a real awareness of feelings in relation to thoughts and situations.

Error-prone thinking

Many of the negative thoughts and feelings that we have about ourselves are caused by what we call cognitive bias – patterns of distorted thinking. Learning to recognize these patterns is a useful skill, as you will then be able to recognize a great many of your individual negative thoughts as one of these thinking styles – and challenging them becomes much easier.

Recognizing distorted thinking is not always easy. We assume that all our thinking is rational and correct even when it is negative. In a good frame of mind, it may be (though not always). But when we are in a poor frame of mind, our thinking can become distorted without our realizing that this is happening.

The problem is that, once we start making thinking errors, we tend to stick with them. They become assumptions and beliefs that we retain, unless we make an effort to recognize them and change them.

Psychologists have identified a number of common thinking errors that most of us make some of the time (and some of us make all of the time). If you know what these are, and can recognize them, it will make your thought-challenging rebuttals much easier to formulate. Read them through and place a tick against any you feel apply to you.

OVERGENERALIZING THE SPECIFIC

You overgeneralize the specific when you come to a general conclusion based on a single incident or piece of evidence. You use words such as 'always' and 'never', 'nobody' and 'everyone', to make an all-embracing rule out of a specific situation. If you make a mistake, you tell yourself that you are hopeless. If you get rejected, you tell yourself that you are unlovable.

Examples
- ▶ You have a minor car accident and you decide you are a dangerous driver (and must never drive again).
- ▶ One failed recipe means you cannot cook and wobbly stitching means you cannot sew.
- ▶ Someone treats you unfairly and you say, 'Nobody likes me.'

MIND-READING

This is one of the commonest thinking errors we make when our self-esteem is low. Without their saying so, we 'know' what people are thinking and why they act the way they do. In particular, we are able to divine how people are feeling towards us. It is fatal to self-esteem because we believe that others agree with our negative opinions of ourselves.

Yet we are jumping to conclusions without any real evidence – and, for some reason, we only seem to have the gift of mind-reading negative views. Interestingly, we never seem to develop a talent for mind-reading positive thoughts!

Examples
- ▶ 'I know he thinks I am boring.'
- ▶ 'I can tell she doesn't like me.'
- ▶ 'I'm sure they don't really want me in their group.'

MAGNIFICATION AND FILTERING

We take the negative details from a situation and then magnify them, while at the same time filtering out all the positive aspects. We focus on the one thing that went badly in an otherwise successful presentation. We dismiss all our achievements and focus bleakly on the one thing that we are not so good at.

Example
- ▶ You have dressed beautifully for a formal evening and your partner or friend pays you the well-deserved compliment, saying how nice you look. However, as you leave the room he or she mentions that the hem of your skirt is not quite straight at the back. You now feel that you no longer look lovely, and that the evening will be spoiled because you will worry about the hem of your dress. The fact that, apart from this, you look stunning quite passes you by.

POLARIZED THINKING

Sometimes called 'all-or-nothing thinking', this is where we think of people, situations or events in extremes – 'I must be perfect or I am a failure', 'If I'm not beautiful, I'm ugly.' There is no middle ground. The problem is that we usually find ourselves at the negative end of our polarized extremes. So if you cannot be all good, you must be all bad.

Examples
- ▶ If you don't get the job you want, your future is ruined.
- ▶ If your relationship doesn't work out, you will never find true love.

CATASTROPHIZING

We expect disaster. We believe that things will almost certainly go wrong if they possibly can – and that, if they do, we will not be able to cope. So that not only do we overestimate the likelihood of calamity, we multiply it by our perceived idea of the catastrophic consequences. Whenever we notice or hear about a problem, we start on 'what ifs' and then decide that, if this terrible thing did happen to us, we would not be able to cope.

Examples
- ▶ 'What if tragedy strikes? I will lose everything and life as I know it will be over.'
- ▶ 'What if it happens to me? Some people might cope, but I know I would not be able to.'
- ▶ 'I know this will turn out badly. It will be just another thing I cannot deal with.'

PERSONALIZATION

This involves thinking that everything people do or say is some kind of reaction to us.

Examples
- ▶ Perhaps your partner mentions that the home is looking a little untidy. You will immediately 'read' this comment as a criticism of your housekeeping skills.
- ▶ Someone mentions that the work team haven't achieved their targets this month. You instantly decide that this comment is really directed at you personally.
- ▶ You find yourself becoming unnecessarily defensive, and possibly even cause ill feeling, by taking someone's passing remark as personal criticism.

BLAMING

This is the opposite of personalization. We hold other people, organizations – or even the universe – responsible for our problems. We feel unable to change our views or our circumstances, as we see ourselves as victims of other people's thoughtlessness and meanness.

Examples
- ▶ 'She has made me feel terrible.'
- ▶ 'That company ruined my life'
- ▶ 'If he hadn't done what he did, I wouldn't have reacted that way.'

SELF-BLAME

In this case, instead of feeling a victim, you feel responsible for the pain and happiness of everyone around you.

Examples
- ▶ If your daughter misses a lift taking her to a special occasion, you feel totally to blame for not having chivvied her along (even though she is 17 and has taken the whole afternoon getting ready).
- ▶ If your firm loses an important client, you will find a way to believe that something you did caused this.

RIGID THINKING

We feel resentful because we think we know what's right, but other people won't agree with us. We continually attempt to prove that our opinions and actions are correct. We expect other people to change their views and actions if we pressure or cajole them enough. We try to change people in this way when we believe our hopes for happiness depend entirely on their behaving differently.

Examples
- ▶ 'I can't understand why people don't see things my way. There must be something wrong with me.'
- ▶ 'I can't understand why people don't see things my way. There must be something wrong with them.'

A positive way forward

While it can be hard to discover that much of your thinking is biased by negative distortions, acknowledging this is the first step to change. The next step is to use this knowledge to help you tackle your thoughts.

… and how?

By working to familiarize yourself with these cognitive distortions.

Once you understand them and can recall them easily, you can begin to spot them when they crop up. They are easier for you to identify than some of your negative thoughts because of the patterns they follow, and you can take an 'Oh, I recognize what I'm doing!' attitude to them and then rethink what has actually happened.

Most people, when presented with these styles of distorted thinking and asked to acknowledge any that apply to them, find themselves actually smiling as they recognize these common thinking errors that most of us make a great deal of the time. They are normal! We all do it. Now you can become more aware of them and knock them on the head quite easily.

In your Stress Journal keep a record of your negative thoughts and, against each thought, write down which cognitive bias applies to it. For example:

Negative thought	Cognitive bias
'I cannot cook at all. My Beef Wellington was so dry.'	Overgeneralizing the specific Polarized thinking
'I know they all thought I was a fool at the meeting.'	Mind-reading
'I wouldn't have acted that way if John had been a bit nicer to me.'	Blaming

A great many of your negative thoughts will fall into one of the categories referred to above. This will make it a great deal easier for you to recognize where you are going wrong with your thinking, and to put it right.

The very familiarity of these thinking errors may be quite comforting to you. Most of us make them at some point or other; many of us quite often. Becoming more aware of them in day-to-day life will give you confidence that you can spot them, challenge them and re-evaluate them without too much difficulty.

Exercise

Pick three stressful situations in the recent past that have triggered negative thinking. Write them down. Now see if you can match those thoughts to any of the above thinking errors.

Once you have done that, 'rethink' the situation in a more rational way and write down those thoughts. Checking out possible thinking errors is another excellent skill to add to your toolbox of skills for closely examining your thinking. Make sure that you use it regularly.

Where's the evidence?

One of the problems people have with challenging negative thinking, and replacing a negative thought with one that is more balanced and helpful, is that the inclination is to still 'really believe' the negative thought.

Negative thoughts can be very hard to shift. It may take a great deal of practice to replace pessimistic beliefs with more constructive ones, and a very helpful tool – thought by many to be the most important 'thought-shifter' around – is to ask a simple question:

> *'If this is really so, where's the evidence?'*

Tom was very stressed at work and was really beginning to feel swamped and unable to cope. When he mentioned this to a colleague, Jim, his advice was to talk to his boss and explain the position. Tom said that he thought he couldn't do this, as he was sure that his boss thought he wasn't up to the job and was looking to find a reason to get rid of him.

Tom felt more stressed than ever. Not only was he totally swamped with work that he felt he could not possibly complete on time, but now he had the worry that he might lose his job if he didn't. The extra stress caused his work rate to slow and more mistakes to appear.

When Jim popped his head round Tom's door he could see that Tom was in despair. 'Stop for a moment, Tom. Let's talk about this.'

'I don't have a moment,' said Tom. 'I'm so behind already and I'll get the sack if I don't finish this tonight.'

'Hold on there,' said Jim. 'Can I just ask you what happened two weeks ago when the sales awards were announced? Can I just ask you whose presentation brought in the biggest new client our company has had this year? And would you please tell me who has been recommended for the senior sales position when Peter retires in six months? Who is that?'

Tom blushed. 'Well, me, I guess,' he said sheepishly.

'And if you were your manager, would you give someone like that the sack, or would you be more likely to listen seriously to their problems and attempt to help them?'

'Well, the latter, I suppose,' said Tom.

'OK, then. What are your plans now?' said Jim.

'I'll speak to my manager,' replied Tom, with a rueful smile. 'Thanks, Jim. You have put things in perspective for me.'

This is what we mean by 'looking for evidence'. Tom's thinking had become so negatively skewed that he was discounting evidence that was staring him (or, at least, his work colleague) in the face which made it clear his thinking was likely to be incorrect. Once he was forced to look for evidence to back up his thinking, he could find little. However, there was a great deal to show that his thinking was incorrect.

Insight

Never accept that your pessimistic thinking is 'spot on'. Always look for evidence to back it up – you may get a surprise when there is less than you think!

Exercise

Write down three situations over the last two weeks (or longer ago if you have had a really good last two weeks) when you have felt especially stressed. Attempt to recall your thinking at those times. Then draw a line down the page and write 'Where's the evidence?' at the top of the right-hand column.

You will be ideally looking for evidence to dispute your negativity. However, don't worry if sometimes you have evidence to support your worries. Coping skills kick in then, and we will be dealing with these later in this book.

Be your own best friend

We don't always have a friend or colleague around to point our thinking into a more positive direction, so a good question to ask yourself in these circumstances is:

'If this was happening to my best friend, rather than to me, what would I say to them? What evidence would I point out to them to help them see that their thoughts or assessment of a situation were not 100-per-cent true?'

The answer you will probably come up with will usually be quite different to your own negative self-talk. We are always so much wiser and more constructive about finding solutions for others than we are for ourselves!

So become your own 'best friend'. Use the question above regularly, and you will find that it will really help you to resolve stressful problems.

If a friend made a statement you felt was possibly skewed – or just plain wrong – you would look at the evidence with them as a natural process. So do this for yourself as well.

ALWAYS CHECK IT OUT!

A question of balance

Unfortunately, when we are suffering from stress and its associated emotions of anxiety or depression, we tend to look for evidence to back up our negative thinking and discount the positive.

If we say 'hello' to a colleague in the corridor at work and they walk past us without responding, in a poor frame of mind we see that as evidence that we are unlikeable or of no consequence. In a good frame of mind we would probably assume that our colleague was simply preoccupied.

So check for evidence to support or dispute your negative thinking. This will help you begin to believe your more positive beliefs more strongly.

Insight
▶ Always advise yourself exactly as though you are advising your best friend. It is the most useful skill.
▶ Get a balance between noticing both positive and negative events in the day, rather than focusing on the bad things.

Exercise
Pick three worries that you currently have – they can be to do with work, relationships, life direction, whatever. Jot them down. Now imagine that your best friend is describing these worries to you.

Write down exactly what you would tell them.

Now, does this give you a new perspective on your problems?

KEEP IN MIND

1 Many people find thought challenging less helpful than they had hoped. This is usually because they are challenging the wrong thought. Pinpointing exactly what the problem is can be quite hard.

2 To ensure that you are not wasting time, it is vital to learn the skills needed to detect the thought that is really troubling you: the stress trigger.

3 A good way of achieving this is to rate both your stress levels (1–100 per cent, say) and the importance of your thought in relation to the stress (again, 1–100 per cent, say). If there is a 'match', then you are likely to have correctly identified the thought causing the stress.

4 Make sure that you understand and use the valuable Downward Arrow technique as an excellent tool for uncovering what is really bothering you.

5 Appreciate that your emotions drive your thinking as powerfully as your thinking drives your emotions.

6 If you have a problem identifying your emotions, simply becoming aware of bodily changes can be helpful – stomach churning or sweating can signal high anxiety, while lethargy and malaise can indicate depression.

7 Cognitive bias refers to patterns of distorted thinking that we are often not aware of. We assume that all our thinking is rational and correct but this is far from true. Become familiar with the most common thinking errors that you make and when you feel stressed, ask yourself which of these errors you might be applying.

8 'Where's the evidence?' is one of the most valuable questions you can ask yourself when disputing negative thinking. You will often be surprised by just how little evidence you have to support your negative thinking – and how much to support a more balanced view.

9 Be your own best friend. Ask yourself what you would say to a friend who had similar problems to yourself and you will find this a good way to resolve those problems yourself.

5

The physical effects of stress and how to deal with them

In this chapter you will learn:
- *how body awareness can help you to beat stress*
- *how to breathe effectively in order to reduce tension*
- *skills to help you relax at will*
- *whether the food in your store cupboard is adding to your stress – and how to change this*
- *how poor sleep can affect you and how to improve it.*

Calming down – but how?

One of the biggest worries of those who are aware that their lives are full of stress is the effect it may have on them physically. We have already discussed the fact that stress can be a contributory factor to certain illnesses. The other side of this coin is that our bodies will work very effectively with us to relieve stress.

In this chapter, therefore, we will be looking at the wide variety of ways we can relieve stress through encouraging our body to help us out.

Recognizing the signs

Let's ensure that you know how to identify the physical effects of stress within your body.

Remember the 'fight-or-flight' mechanism that we discussed in Chapter 2. Our muscles contract and become tense under orders from the brain, which, in prehistoric times, was telling the body to prepare to fight a tiger (or run like the wind away from one). So the tension was intended to be helpful to you – to keep you safer in dangerous situations.

The problem with messages between brain and body is that they tend to be very simple – just a sort of 'red alert' really, with a flashing light that has 'DANGER' written on it in big, bold letters. The body doesn't get told what the 'danger' is, and therefore reacts in its pre-programmed way – ready to fight a tiger – even when the stressful event is nothing more than a disgruntled shop assistant being rude to you, or you miss your train by a whisker.

The muscular tension that you feel is the same.

Insight
▶ Muscular tension is the body's response to 'danger' signals from the brain.
▶ Somehow or other, our bodies still operate on the old 'sabre-toothed tiger in the bushes' premise. So don't be alarmed by the initial physical symptoms that arise with stress and anxiety. They are not harmful (unless perhaps you have a cardiac condition).

Exercise
Think about times that you feel especially stressed. What physical symptoms do you notice? These vary for each of us, but jot down those that you encounter regularly – this might include tightness in your stomach, your heart racing, shortness of breath, sweating, dizziness, clammy hands...

Learn to be aware of tension

Learning to recognize the bodily tension we referred to in the last chapter is the first step to releasing it. Here is an exercise that will help you do this:

Copy out the schedule below (Table 5.1), and fill it in on a daily basis for a week. We'll call this your **tension awareness record**, and we give you some examples to start you off.

Now construct your own diary, and keep it for a week. Develop an awareness of any patterns you find.

Table 5.1   Tension awareness record

Date ....

Time	Stressor	Physical reaction
7.30 a.m.	Train is cancelled	Tenseness in neck and shoulders
11.15 a.m.	Manager asks to see me regarding work I know I have done badly	Tightness in stomach
2.45 p.m.	Huge amount of paperwork to deal with by 5 p.m.	Slight headache
4.45 p.m.	Can see will not get away in time for reasonable train	Headache worsens
6.00 p.m.	Race to station. Train packed to eyeballs. No seats. Am not going to get home in time to get to parents' evening.	Pounding headache Tightness in stomach

Different events cause different tensions

You will notice that certain events – for example, personal confrontations – trigger tension in your stomach. Events that trigger irritability – caused, for example by too heavy a workload – tend to produce tension in the head, leading to headaches.

Once you become used to being aware of the types of tension you feel, and when and why you feel them, you have the opportunity of using one of the many skills you are learning to reduce the stress to manageable proportions, or even eliminate it altogether.

Exercise

Fill in your tension awareness record for today. Take a look at the situations that caused tension, and the type of tension that they cause. Can you see any links?

Breathe...!

Yes, we know. If you have got this far in the book, you already do! But what do you breathe for?

We suspect that most of you have simply answered that question with:

'To stay alive' (or words to that effect).

While we agree that staying alive is integral to wellbeing, and that breathing to achieve this is important, if that's all you think it achieves, you are missing out on all the other things that breathing can do for you.

What other things?

Exercise

Let's see what you think. Place a sheet of paper over the next part of this chapter, and on a further sheet of paper jot down any ideas that you have about the benefits of effective breathing.

If you got as far as three, then you have done very well.

Now take a look at all the many positives of breathing well:

▶ It carries oxygen into our bloodstream. The bloodstream, in turn, acts rather like a mobile grocery van, moving round the various parts of our bodies and providing them with amounts of the nutrients that they need to keep healthy.

▶ It carries oxygen to our brains. Want to think faster, at a higher level? Breathe better!

- It keeps our heart rate and blood pressure down.
- If you have studied yoga, you will have heard of the 'calming breath' – the idea that breathing is good for your soul as well as your body.
- And did you know that oxygen also scares cancer cells? They hate oxygen!
- And most importantly – for the purposes of managing stress:

BREATHING HELPS YOU TO RELAX

Insight
Breathing does a great deal more for us than simply keep us alive.

Exercise
Whatever time of the day or evening you are reading this, simply begin to have more awareness of your breathing.

Do you find that this awareness slows your breathing down at all? (If not, don't worry – you will learn how to achieve this.)

SO WHAT'S NOT HAPPENING? WHY AM I STILL STRESSED?

Well, like many things in life, there is a good way to breathe and a bad way to breathe.

Many of us do it the bad way!

This is because breathing is second nature: it just 'happens' and we don't waste too much time thinking about it or taking notice of the way we do it.

So here's the first item we want you to do – start noticing how you breathe.

CHECKING IT OUT

When you have a quiet moment (if you're reading this on the train, just book mark this page and come back to it), check this out:

- Find a bit of space somewhere and lie on the floor on your back, with your knees slightly bent, in a relaxing position.
- Place your right hand on your stomach, just where your waistline is.

- ▶ Place your left hand in the centre of your chest.
- ▶ Now, without changing your natural rhythm, simply breathe in and out, and look out for the hand that rises highest when you breathe in – is it your right hand (on your stomach) or your left hand (on your chest)?

This will tell you, in simple terms, whether you are a deep breather (when the hand on your stomach will lift the highest) or a shallow breather (when the hand on your chest will rise higher).

ERROR MESSAGES THAT TRICK OUR BODIES

Returning to the fight-or-flight analogy again, if we are going to run like the wind or fight to the death, our muscles need a lot of oxygen. So when our bodies get the 'red alert' signal from our brains, that is their goal. They achieve it by getting the oxygenated blood round our bodies at a really fast pace – no time to be lost – and to do this, our bodies ask our hearts to 'increase the pump rate'. How do we speed up the heart rate? We speed up our breathing. How do we breathe more quickly? We breathe more shallowly.

Instead of taking deep, full breaths that come up from our diaphragm, we breathe in and out very quickly, using just the upper part of our chest.

Stress, anxiety, panic attacks, headaches, muscle tension and fatigue are all exacerbated by quick, shallow breathing.

Insight
- ▶ Good breathing relaxes us; bad breathing stresses us.
- ▶ It is therefore vital to learn to breathe well.

Exercise
Become aware of your breathing when you are a) in a stressful situation and b) relaxing. Notice whether it gets deeper or shallower, faster or slower. When in the day is your breathing at its absolute slowest?

Learning to breathe well

Of the many skills we teach our clients to reduce the physical symptoms of stress and anxiety, quite a number of them tell us that learning to control their breathing has been the most powerful of all.

If you really can only do one simple thing to make a difference, we would recommend that this be it.

You need to know how to breathe so brilliantly that you will be able, at will, to...

▶ easily release muscular tension
▶ become so relaxed you will have trouble staying awake
▶ dramatically reduce distressing symptoms associated with anxiety states
▶ feel more energized and up to speed

...and it isn't hard.

THE EASY WAY FIRST

Don't get wound up trying to do this exercise perfectly. You want to end up feeling really comfortable, not getting stressed out even further from counting breaths, wondering if they were long enough, short enough or just plain enough of them.

You are looking to 'feel' your breathing relax your body – and you will know when it happens. Many experts will tell you, 'Count to 4', 'Count to 6', 'Count to 8'. This is not only confusing, but can lead some people to hyperventilate. So our advice is to find a count that fits for you and within which you can feel a rhythm that is comfortable and breathing that is slow and deep. Whatever works for you is fine.

HORIZONTAL OR VERTICAL?

Another option about which we feel you should decide for yourself is whether to sit down or lie down. You are most welcome to lie down if you prefer. However, our preference would be for you to sit, as our goal for you is for you to be able to use this skill 'whenever and wherever', and finding a place to lie down when you're in a meeting or working in an open-plan office is not realistic. (Also, if you lie down, you increase your chances of falling off to sleep – unless that genuinely is your goal, of course.)

Let's have a go:

▶ Get your hands out again, and place them in the same positions as before (check back if you have forgotten).
▶ Now breathe in slowly through your nose).

- ▶ Ensure as you do this that the hand on your stomach rises, and the hand on your chest moves as little as possible.
- ▶ Now exhale slowly (count again if this helps you) and as you do, feel the hand on your stomach gently fall back.

This is a simple breathing technique that you can use whenever you like.

Insight
Learning to breathe well isn't difficult – but is perhaps one of the most important skills you can use to reduce the physical symptoms of stress.

Exercise
Please set aside 15 minutes to practise the simple breathing exercise we have just outlined.

This is to get you used to breathing in this way – we won't ask you to devote this much time on a daily basis.

WHAT DOES 'WHENEVER I LIKE' MEAN?

One of the weaknesses of skills such as good breathing is that all people feel they have to do is to simply use them in a crisis. 'Manager sends memo round saying important meeting this afternoon regarding complete restructuring of company' sounds like a good time to practise your breathing skills. Well, yes and no.

Insight
For instant stress reduction – which is what you are looking for – you need to practise breathing on a daily basis.

If you wait for a crisis, you are not going to be skilled enough, or practised enough, to be able to use this tool on an almost unconscious, second-nature basis. You're going to have to run through the above steps in your mind, try to remember what and in which order you do them all and, whoops! ...too late, you're all wound up and in the manager's office.

You would not expect to be able to get the ball into the net at football (hockey, lacrosse, whatever) in the microsecond that you have to make the shot before being tackled, without it being quite automatic... and it becomes automatic because you have practised it a *thousand* times. You don't have (or have the time) to think about it.

A GOOD RULE

A good rule is the 'Rule of Four' – devised not because of its absolute optimum effectiveness (although it pretty well is) but simply because it is easy to remember:

- ▶ Breathe in and out to a count of four.
- ▶ Do this for four minutes.
- ▶ Do it four times a day.

To explain...

- ▶ Four is a 'middle of the road' number for counting breaths in and out, so handy to use.
- ▶ Practising four times a day is also obvious – the more you do it, the better.
- ▶ Doing it for four minutes actually has a lot going for it – it is not just a number picked out of thin air. To give your lungs a chance to do the job of getting the new oxygen into the capillaries that feed your circulatory system, and to remove the stale carbon dioxide that needs getting rid of, takes around four minutes.

Insight
- ▶ Don't wait for a crisis – good breathing skills need to be second nature.
- ▶ Which means... regular practice.

> **Exercise**
> Using the Rule of Four, start building this into your daily routine. You are learning now to make good breathing your normal breathing, rather than simply 'crisis breathing'.

Don't fool yourself (or us)

Occasionally, when we ask clients to use breathing to relieve stress, they will say to us: 'Tried that. It didn't work.' What we find in these instances is that the client will then go on to tell us they 'tried it' for 'two minutes' (not really long enough), and that the reality is that their idea of two minutes is more likely to be 30 seconds. We will usually also then find that 'tried it' means 'tried it *once*'.

If good, deep, relaxed breathing is not reducing your stress and anxiety levels at all, then perhaps...

1 you have not done it often enough, *and*
2 you have not done it for long enough.

There is a great deal more that we could teach you about advanced breathing techniques, but we don't have the space within the confines of this book. However, do consider finding out more about advanced breathing techniques either via the Internet, specialized books, or taking yoga or meditation classes. You will find these skills extremely helpful in your quest to reduce the physical symptoms of stress.

Insight
▶ Good breathing will relax you, ease muscular tension and diminish other physical symptoms of stress.
▶ Good breathing is not difficult to master, but it does require regular practice.

Exercise
Make sure that, by the end of today, you have practised these breathing skills at least twice. Then, using the Rule of Four, for the first week diarize it and write down the times at which you practised, on a daily basis. After that, use the Rule of Four on a regular basis.

Relaxing to reduce stress

Probably the most common phrase we hear from friends and colleagues when we begin to look frazzled round the edges and steam is coming out of our ears is 'Just relax!' Yet in the midst of a frantic day at work, or stuck in a ten-mile tailback when we should have been somewhere important half an hour ago, we may well wonder: how does that work?

Well, perhaps surprisingly, it can, and we will teach you now to relax AT WILL.

When we teach breathing skills to aid the physical symptoms of stress, we always teach relaxation skills as well. Together, these two techniques form an extremely effective barrier to stress, or – if stress has already crept up on you – will reduce it speedily and dramatically.

First, the easy way.

YOUR NUMBER ONE SIMPLEST RELAXATION TECHNIQUE...

Would you believe – it's yawning! While we tend to think yawning simply indicates tiredness or boredom, on many occasions it is actually helping to relieve stress. The reason for this is that it ensures more oxygen enters our lungs and moves into our bloodstream, de-tensing muscles and de-stressing our brains.

So if you feel a yawn coming on, and you have enough privacy, don't stifle it – use it as the ultra-deep breath that it is and let it flow right through you.

(NB: Not advisable for use at dinner parties or promotion board meetings.)

Unless you live on a desert island, you will have spent many hours reading magazine and newspaper articles as well as books and Internet articles on how to relax. Possibly, you already have a relaxation routine – if this is the case, move on. If not, you may be confused by the number of different approaches to relaxation. These can include:

▶ lying on a mat thinking about faraway places
▶ playing an audiotape of someone speaking to you in a soothing voice
▶ making your own tape
▶ listening to the sounds of waves or jungle noises.

If any of these work for you, that's wonderful and we encourage you to continue with whatever helps you relax. However, a weakness of these methods can be that you cannot use them *at will*. It takes time and privacy to attend to this type of relaxation, so if this is a problem for you we will now teach you how to overcome this.

Insight
▶ Relaxation and breathing together will dramatically reduce the physical symptoms of stress.
▶ Use a yawn as a simple 'relaxer'.

RELAXATION SKILLS

While some of the relaxation solutions listed earlier may work well for you, our experience with clients has shown us that they get a more immediate and visible benefit from using muscle-relaxation techniques. We therefore recommend that you use these, as they have the huge advantage of being able to relax you very quickly and in almost any situation.

Insight
Progressive muscle relaxation involves tensing and relaxing, in succession, 13 different muscle groups of the body.

The idea is to tense each muscle group hard for about ten seconds, and then let go of it suddenly, enjoying the sensation of limpness. Allow the relaxation to develop for at least 15–20 seconds before going on to the next group of muscles. Notice how the muscle group feels when relaxed, in contrast to how it felt when tensed. You might also say to yourself, 'Relax', as you do so. Make sure you are in a setting that is quiet and comfortable and take a few slow, deep breaths before you start.

To begin with, do this with all 13 muscle groups. This will take about 20 minutes. You will almost certainly find that you prefer some more than others – that is, you get a greater 'feel good' factor. So pick your eight favourites.

The eventual goal of these exercises is to teach you to relax at will.

Do these every day for a week. At the end of the week, pick the best four. For the next week, do these four every day. Then pick your best two. Do these two every day for a week. Now you have the option of keeping two up your sleeve, or reducing to one firm favourite.

This 'favourite' will be the relaxation exercise that allows you to relax at will and quite instantaneously. Any time. Any place.

Along with deep breathing, you now have two tools that you can use easily and anywhere to bring down your stress levels physically.

Here are two simple exercises to start you off:

1 Clench your fists. Hold for ten seconds... and then release for about 15–20 seconds.
2 Tighten your biceps by drawing your forearms up toward your shoulders and 'making a muscle' with both arms. Hold for about ten seconds... and then relax for 15–20 seconds.

Insight
Tensing and then relaxing your muscles is a very powerful form of relaxation.

Exercise
Practise the two exercises above. Do each of them several times to give yourself the idea of tensing and relaxing. Feel the relaxation flow through your body.

You may find this hard at first, but keep practising until it becomes easier – it will!

MORE MUSCLE-RELAXATION EXERCISES

Now that you have practised one or two of the exercises, here are the rest. Try them all out, and pick your eight favourites to continue with. Remember that, for each exercise, hold for ten seconds and relax for 15–20 seconds.

▶ Tighten the muscles on the undersides of your upper arms by extending your arms out straight and locking your elbows. Hold... then relax.
▶ Tighten your forehead muscles by raising your eyebrows as high as you can. Hold... then relax.
▶ Open your mouth so widely that you stretch the muscles around the hinges of your jaw. Hold... then relax. Let your lips part and let your jaw hang loose.
▶ Screw up the muscles around your eyes, clenching them tightly shut. Hold... then relax.
▶ Tighten the muscles in the back of your neck by gently pulling your head way back, as if you were going to touch your back with your head. Focus only on tensing your neck muscles. Hold... then relax.

► Tighten your shoulders by raising them up as if you were going to touch your ears. Hold… then relax.

► Tighten the muscles around your shoulder blades by pushing your shoulder blades back as if you were going to touch them together. Hold… then relax.

► Tighten the muscles of your chest by taking in a deep breath. Hold for up to ten seconds… and then release slowly.

► Tighten your stomach muscles by sucking your stomach in. Hold… and then release. Imagine a wave of relaxation spreading through your abdomen.

► Tighten your lower back by arching it up. (Omit this exercise if you have lower back pain.) Hold… then relax.

► Tighten your buttocks by pulling them together. Hold… then relax. Imagine the muscles in your hips going loose and limp.

► Squeeze the muscles of your thighs all the way down to your knees. Hold… then relax. Feel your thigh muscles smoothing out and relaxing completely.

► Tighten your feet by curling your toes downward. Hold… then relax.

► Finally, imagine a wave of relaxation slowly spreading throughout your body, starting at your head and gradually penetrating every muscle group all the way down to your toes.

Insight
Using these exercises will result in you being able to relax quickly and at will.

You now need to follow the instructions we gave you earlier in the chapter and continue with these exercises for four weeks until you can use one or two exercises to relax yourself in an instant.

Getting physical – is exercise a part of your life?

As we have said before, we appreciate that, for some of you, certain chapters in this book will be unnecessary, as you are already either doing the right thing, or at least know what to do and have a plan.

However, we never cease to be amazed by the number of people we meet who, when we question them about what exercise they do, say, 'Er, none.'

Exercise is good for me because:	Exercise I take per week (type, time spent):

FEELING GOOD

Many of you, we suspect, will have listed things such as 'staying healthy' and 'the feel good factor' in the first column. You are quite right, of course, but you will be more motivated to exercise, and appreciate its positive impact better, if you are more specifically aware of more of its benefits. Exercise...

▶ decreases your blood pressure
▶ lowers your heart rate
▶ slows your breathing
▶ keeps essential muscle groups in good shape
▶ keeps weight down (which, in turn, helps prevent diseases of obesity such as diabetes, strokes, etc.)
▶ keeps energy levels up
▶ oxygenates your body, keeping your blood and circulation healthy
▶ actively increases production of serotonin – the 'feel good' chemical that is nature's natural antidepressant
▶ reduces stress, not only via all of the above, but by re-channelling your energy into something constructive for your wellbeing.

Insight
Imprint these on your heart (or pin a copy to your fridge). They are your motivators.

SO WHAT DO YOU DO?

If you don't already have a great exercise programme, the question becomes more, 'What *could* you do?' Only you can decide on the best form of exercise for yourself – What sports do you like? Is there a gym nearby? – we urge you to build two things into whatever you choose:

1 **Timing:** ideally, 30 minutes three times a week where your heart rate rises above its normal level.
2 **Consistency:** don't create a programme that exhausts you, takes over your week, and that you give up after a month. Make sure that, whatever you do, it is sustainable – you need to be thinking of exercise for life.

SOME EASY OPTIONS

We can hear the objection some of you are making already: 'I'm stressed enough already owing to lack of time. Now you are asking me to make more time!' Well, yes, we are. Sorry. It's too important. But here are some easy options that you may be discounting:

1 Stairs are your friends! Never take a lift unless it's absolutely necessary.
2 If you drive to work, can you park a little further away from your office? If so, do, and walk the rest of the way.
3 If your workplace happens to be within walking distance – and that means up to half an hour's walking distance – then, once or twice a week, leave the car at home.
4 Not enough time for that? Get a bike. Use it whenever you can.
5 Sack the gardener.
6 Pick a half-hour TV programme you really enjoy, and plan a small exercise routine that you can do while watching.

Insight
▶ Exercise is VITAL.
▶ It is a huge stress-reducer.
▶ Consistency is the key.

Exercise
Unless you already exercise regularly, devise an exercise plan that has the following attributes:

86

> ▶ Where possible, it involves doing something you like.
> ▶ It will raise your heart rate.
> ▶ You will do it regularly – ideally, three times per week.
> ▶ You will take a long-term view, and your plan will incorporate the ability to sustain at least something along the same lines on a permanent basis.

You are what you eat

When you are feeling really stressed, rushed, late, have too much to do, or just cannot hang on to the situation – what do you choose to eat:

▶ nothing?

▶ a chocolate bar?

▶ whatever is in your desk drawer at the time, even if it is just a two-day-old sandwich?

▶ a takeaway sent in from the curry house / fish and chip shop / pizza outlet next door?

If you consider yourself to be a smart, healthy eater, feel free to move on. However, if you feel too stressed to worry about what you are eating, and if you said 'yes' to any of the boxes above, then you need to know that what you eat is actually *contributing* to the stress in your life, not relieving it.

THE FOOD–MOOD RELATIONSHIP

In recent years, much more attention has been paid to the relationship between food and mood. We are currently eating the most stressful diet ever known. Junk food may be easily available and seem the answer when we are 'on the run', but it can add to your stress levels.

For example, that comforting chocolate bar will give you a 'feel good' factor – for a short while. The sugar in the bar increases your blood sugar levels and gives you instant energy. But wait for half an hour and you will feel more tired than ever – as your blood sugar level subsequently plummets to a new, lower level. This 'up and down' of blood sugar levels is disastrous for both your body and your brain. Stress increases. You feel worse than ever.

However, change is not too difficult, and we will make suggestions that you can incorporate into a hectic lifestyle. Here they are:

Remember: Following these guidelines will REDUCE your stress levels.

▶ Reduce (or eliminate altogether if you are very strong-willed) all sweet, sugary foods. It really is not too strong a statement to say that sugar is, under normal circumstances, a *poison*. It does you no earthly good at all, and your energy levels will be much better sustained by the alternatives below.

▶ We don't mean to blind you with science, but you do need to know what 'complex carbohydrates' are, because they can enhance your performance under stress by releasing energy consistently and slowly. You will find them in, for example, bran- and oat-based cereals, wholemeal bread and pasta, and brown rice. Portion-wise, think in terms of an amount the size of a tennis ball on a daily basis.

▶ Eat one or two good helpings of protein daily. Get it from fish, chicken or lean meat. If you are a vegetarian or vegan, soya and tofu are good alternatives. These foods will really improve your mental functioning, and supply essential cell-repairing amino acids. With regards to the amount, an easy rule of thumb is that your daily protein intake should be the size of a deck of playing cards.

▶ You would have to live on another planet not to be aware of the 'Eat more fruit and vegetables' campaign. Ideally raw, steamed or lightly cooked, vegetables will provide your body with a host of stress-busting vitamins and nutrients. A good rule-of-thumb is the darker the colour, the better it will be for you. Start with broccoli – truly a 'superfood' and renowned as a cancer preventative if a small amount is eaten daily.

▶ Eat dairy products in moderation. While high in fat, they also provide protein, calcium and potassium, which are all excellent stress-reducers and muscle relaxers.

ON-THE-RUN SNACKING

A few suggestions:

▶ any piece of fruit (bananas are especially popular and easy to eat – you can even buy plastic 'banana cases' now to prevent them getting squashed!)

- ► a handful of nuts
- ► a low-fat yoghurt (natural, unsweetened, if you can bear it)
- ► a cereal bar made from natural ingredients only (check the packaging – don't assume that all cereal bars are healthy)
- ► rice crackers
- ► a piece of Edam or Gouda cheese (lower in calories than Cheddar)
- ► a tub of cottage cheese (there are tasty varieties available)
- ► a chicken drumstick
- ► crab sticks.

You will find lots more ideas once you start looking.

Exercise

Make a list of healthy snacks that appeal to you. Then hit the supermarket and ensure that you have good stocks of these items.

Look back over the last week at what you ate. Write down what you now recognize as 'bad stuff'. Write down any 'good stuff' (from the above list). What changes can you make to ensure that you ditch stress-enhancing foods and focus on stress-reducing foods?

The Land of Nod... or wakefulness?

Poor sleep patterns can be a symptom of stress. They can also be a cause of stress.

Take the sleep quiz below to see if sleep is a problem for you...

Sleep quiz

How many of the following statements apply to you?

- ▶ I wake up in the morning feeling as tired as when I went to bed.
- ▶ I never wake ahead of my alarm clock.
- ▶ I always wake an hour or more ahead of my alarm clock and cannot return to sleep.
- ▶ It takes me ages to get to sleep at night.
- ▶ I wake several times in the night.
- ▶ I rarely sleep more than two or three hours at a stretch.
- ▶ I usually feel really tired by mid-afternoon.
- ▶ I often wake up at 3 a.m. or 4 a.m. and can't get back to sleep easily.

If you ticked two or more boxes, or any one box where this is a regular occurrence, then you need to develop a sleep routine to reduce the stress that is being created by lack of it.

The following will help:

RESET YOUR BODY CLOCK

Your body clock is a very simple mechanism. Without routine it simply goes haywire. Here is the bad news: tempting though it might be, if you have lain awake for much of the night, tossing, turning and worrying, you still need to get up at exactly the same time every day. Your body needs regularity and consistency to correct itself. So if you feel sleep-deprived, don't stay in bed longer to recuperate – even at weekends. Your body will learn to take the extra sleep it needs at the end of the day, rather than at the beginning, and you will become less of a 'toss and turn' victim.

This is hard. No one likes doing it this way, but it is essential to recalibrate the body.

Insight

Oversleeping is as bad for you, if not worse, than not getting enough sleep. It will make you lethargic and depressed. Don't do it!

BED = SLEEP

Your mind needs to learn that bedtime does not equal reading, watching TV, doing the crossword, texting friends, etc.

BEDTIME = SLEEP TIME!

If you want to do any of the above, do them before you go to bed, not in or from your bed.

GET COMFY

How comfortable is your bed? You won't enjoy a good night's sleep on a lumpy mattress, one that's too hard or too soft. Invest in a new one.

AM I GETTING ENOUGH SLEEP?

Don't lie awake worrying about this. Anything between six and nine hours falls within the 'normal' range. More or less than this occasionally is also OK. More or less than this regularly suggests you need to look at what is going wrong. Recent research has shown that too much sleep is not good for our health. While eight hours used to be regarded as optimum, this has now been reduced to seven hours – with very recent studies showing that people who take only six hours per night actually live longer than those who sleep more.

The overall message here is: don't worry about the amount of sleep you are getting as long as they are within these parameters. It will be perfectly adequate for you.

GETTING TO SLEEP MINDFULLY

The concept of mindfulness has been shown to aid sleep patterns very positively. Mindfulness is a complex subject, but its essence is to bring your mind into the present moment, away from its backward ruminations and forward worrying. So when you lie awake in bed in the early hours, simply 'tune out' and focus on the warmth of the bed, the softness of the pillows, the relaxedness of your muscles – and the fact that (as, again, new research shows) resting is as good for your body as actual sleep. With you no longer actively worrying about sleep or your problems, a mindful approach will help you to drift off naturally or at least stay awake peacefully.

HOW WARM DO YOU NEED TO BE?

For the best sleep, you want to have warm covers, but a cool room. Unless you fear burglars, some ventilation is good.

WAKE NATURALLY

Ditch the blackout curtains. Natural light will gradually reduce the sleep hormone, melatonin, and you will give yourself the chance to wake slowly and naturally, which is much less stressful than a shrill alarm call. Just give it a go for a few nights and see if there is a difference.

MAKE YOUR BEDROOM INVITING

There is no joy in climbing into bed over heaps of clothes, clutter and hobby-related items. If you can create a tranquil environment, your mind will absorb this and bedtime will become something you actually look forward to.

LATE-EVENING CALMING ROUTINES

Develop a relaxing routine for the latter part of the evening. No drinking, smoking, exercising, stressful discussions, television news, scary movies or general rushing around preparing for the next day should take place within one and a half hours of going to bed. Not always possible, we appreciate, but an ideal to aim for if you are taking good sleep seriously.

3 A.M. WAKING

Here you have an option. Either a) get up, go and make a warm drink, watch a bit of TV, read, or whatever, or b) do some relaxation and deep breathing as you lie in bed, at the same time telling yourself that just lying and relaxing is almost as good as sleeping. Earlier in this chapter we highlighted breathing exercises that can help you to relax and switch off. If you cannot stop yourself worrying, then pick the first option. In addition, use the mindfulness exercise described above.

POWER-NAPPING

If you get the chance of a brief 'nap' in the day, take it, but don't make it longer than 15–20 minutes at most, or you will simply feel groggy and disoriented. Many top businesspeople do this regularly, to boost their alertness before important events. Even just a quick five-minute power-nap can really help to revitalize you.

Insight
- ▶ Poor sleep can be both a symptom and a cause of stress.
- ▶ You don't have to put up with poor sleep – have a go at any or all of the above suggestions to improve things.
- ▶ Don't 'oversleep' to compensate.
- ▶ Are you consuming too much caffeine in coffee or tea?

Exercise
Start keeping a written sleep record. You will need to do this for at least two weeks, possibly longer. Note patterns in wakefulness and what may have caused them – late nights out, lack of routine, alcohol, not being comfortable, the room being too hot/cold, etc. You can then use this sleep diary to make appropriate adjustments, using any or all of the positive suggestions above. See what works for you, and keep adjusting until you get a good result.

KEEP IN MIND

1 The negative effect on our physical health is a common and understandable worry when we are stressed, so it is important to understand what the physical symptoms we feel actually mean and why they arise.

2 Appreciate that your body is simply trying to help you when your heart starts pounding or your stomach starts churning. No harm will come to you: it is simply your body's way of positively reacting to the 'danger' message it has received from your brain.

3 Learn to be aware of bodily tension so that you can relate it to what is actually going on for you when you feel this way. Keeping a daily tension awareness record is a good way to achieve this.

4 Good breathing is vital to reducing stress. It does far more than simply keep us alive and one of its many attributes is that good breathing can relax you and reduce stress. It eases muscular tension and helps you to feel more energized and able to cope.

5 Practise breathing exercises on a regular (ideally daily) basis so that they become second nature to you. Don't simply wait for a crisis because you will not be familiar enough with the skill.

6 Common advice others give us to reduce stress is: 'Relax!' However, you need to learn and practise proper relaxation techniques rather than hope for the best. These techniques involve tensing and relaxing various muscle groups in your body. Again, practise on a regular basis.

7 Physical exercise is vital in reducing stress, so if you don't exercise regularly already, find something you like and build it into your daily life.

8 You are what you eat. Poor eating habits can contribute to stress, so review yours and ensure that you are eating healthily. If you are uncertain what would be best, then it is worth paying for a nutritional consultation to get you a healthy eating plan that is tailored to your needs.

9 Sleep – or lack of it – is a common problem when we are stressed. If you have sleep problems, then look at our suggestions for getting over them. If they are having a serious negative impact, then contact a sleep clinic for some expert advice.

6

....

De-stressing through organization

In this chapter you will learn:
- *to reduce stress by improving your organizational skills*
- *to use your most precious commodity – time – effectively*
- *the importance and principles of goal setting*
- *how to reduce your stress-inducing cluttered lifestyle*
- *how prioritizing and delegating will reduce stress.*

Are you (dis)organized?

Do you feel that you are permanently in a state of chaos? Do you look around at piles of paperwork, turn up on the wrong day for appointments, have no clue as to where you would find your bank statements or utility bills?

Are you one the of the many people who purchase extended warranties for electrical goods, only to have no idea at all where the warranty is when the appliance breaks down and you need it?

If so, you are not alone. Frustrating though it is, not being a Totally Organized Person (TOP) is quite normal. (In fact, we find TOPs rather smug and infuriating, and we suspect you may as well.) However, there is a middle way, and you will need to find it if feeling and being disorganized is causing you great stress.

Why do think you are disorganized? Take a look at the following statements, and ask yourself whether they apply to you:

▶ 'I just don't know what to do to become an organized person.'

▶ 'I do know how to become an organized person, but it is all such an effort.'
▶ 'If I had more time, I would be really well organized.'
▶ 'Having some space would make the difference, but there's nowhere for me to put stuff.'
▶ 'It is impossible to get organized with my lifestyle – it's too complex and erratic.'

How many applied to you? If you can truthfully answer 'none', you can skip this entire chapter of the book. However, the likelihood is that, if you feel stressed, you will feel disorganized. In this chapter we will take a look at how to make changes that will streamline your life.

Consider the following three issues:

▶ **Clutter:** Is it everywhere? Does it overwhelm you?
▶ **Lack of time:** Do you really feel that you are doing too much, or are you not organizing your time well enough?
▶ **Goal setting:** Do you stumble along in a crisis-driven way, reacting rather than being proactive? Does this hinder your progress?

Now ask yourself a very important question:

At what point does disorganization really hinder me?

The answer is different for all of us. We know top businesspeople who run successful organizations with offices that look like rubbish tips. We know people who live in pristine environments whose lives are still very stressful – being perfect all the time can be very time-consuming.

You will have your own optimum organizational threshold, and you alone will know what this is. So the advice you will find in this chapter is for you to apply to yourself on an 'as it suits me', rather than a 'one size fits all', basis.

Insight
▶ Lack of organization is a great contributor to stress.
▶ However, finding your own disorganization threshold is important; otherwise achieving something you don't really care about will stress you out even more!

Get yourself motivated

If you are going to make any organizational changes, you have got to...

▶ really *want* to do it, *or*
▶ have a big enough incentive to *make* you do it.

Think about a less stressful life. You are learning that there are many, many ways of reducing stress, but failing to address being more organized will leave a big hole in these ideas.

Where your effort ratings are *above* 7, you will have good motivation to change. Where they are *under* 7, you may need some incentives.

For example:

▶ **Reward yourself:** You could reward yourself for getting a job done by a certain date. Perhaps a pair of theatre tickets for a show you want to see, or a sporting event you are keen on. It works with children, and we really should use it a lot more as adults.
▶ **...Or pay a price:** Sometimes, however, a penalty can be a great incentive as well. Tell yourself you don't get to go out on Friday evening unless your desk at home (or work, or whatever) is tidy and up to date. Stick to it. This might be easier if you get your partner to be firm with you when you weaken.

- **Talk about it:** The more people you tell about your plans, the more likely you are to follow them through. (Shame is a great motivator.)
- **Use embarrassment:** In fact, using shame can be a helpful tool for getting organized at home. Invite some guests over around the time you plan to finish clearing up your living area and you will have excellent motivation to stick with it.
- **Schedule it:** We usually attend appointments that we have in our diaries. Use this 'appointment system' to build in time for getting organized. Schedule two hours, for example on Saturday morning, for clearing out the garage. This will work a great deal better than simply 'planning to find the time at some point'.

Insight
- Work out what motivates you best, and use this to get more organized in specific areas.
- Tell as many people as possible about your plans. Ask them to help you stick to them.

Overcoming procrastination

Most of us procrastinate some of the time. Where we have a task ahead of us…

- that is unpleasant
- with which we don't believe we can deal, *and*
- about whose outcome we are pessimistic

…we become experts in finding a host of tasks to do that *must* be done first. On other occasions, we simply have so many tasks to deal with that we become 'frozen' with indecision, and find it almost impossible to make a start on anything at all.

If any of the above rings bells with you, you are probably a good procrastinator, and – as a result – live with the chronic stress that failing to deal with things in good time brings with it.

'DISPLACEMENT ACTIVITY' (PROCRASTINATION IN DISGUISE)

What happens when something you are finding really hard to tackle has a deadline beginning to tick away? Are any of the following activities ones that you suddenly find a need to undertake:

- ► a major desk or drawer tidy-up?
- ► a session deleting unwanted emails?
- ► sharpening your pencils?
- ► having a quick game of solitaire on the computer?
- ► making endless cups of coffee?
- ► checking every few minutes or so for new emails / text messages?
- ► doodling?
- ► making a long 'to do' list and working on the most unimportant items on the list?

THE ILLUSION OF USEFULNESS

The only reason that procrastination seems to help is that it prevents us from focusing on the main task, thus temporarily reducing our stress levels. However, as the time ticks away, stress levels rise even higher when the task moves no further forward to completion.

FIGHT IT

Your stress levels will rise and rise, the more time you waste staring out of the window or unbending paperclips. So get active, and make yourself overcome procrastination. Here are some suggestions:

- ► **Build in a reward:** 'Once I have done this task, I will treat myself to…'
- ► **Break the task down into small steps:** For example, if you have the whole house to clean, adopt a 'one room a day' approach. Don't think of the whole project, but just what you can easily achieve within your time frame.
- ► **Write your plan down:** Work out how much time you need for each stage, add half as much again, and then leave extra time for unforeseen difficulties. Having more time than you need will help you relax, and actually work faster and more effectively.
- ► **Stop worrying ahead of time:** Save your energies for when you actually have to do the task, and, if you find yourself ruminating ahead of time, silently shout 'STOP!' in your head and refocus on something else.
- ► **Challenge negative thoughts and beliefs:** Don't simply give yourself permission to have thoughts such as 'I'll never get this right', 'I cannot complete the task in the time', 'I've so much to do I can't think straight.' Find positive alternatives to these thoughts. (Reread the earlier chapters of this book if you need to.)

- **Prioritize and stick to your list:** Don't allow yourself to get distracted until you have completed as much as you need to of what is at the top of your list. You will gradually become comfortable with the idea that 'other things can wait'. You will find that they can, and nothing terrible happens.

Insight
- Procrastination is the enemy of stress reduction as it puts even more pressure on our limited time and resources.
- We need to employ a variety of tactics to keep procrastination at bay, and to work hard at these.

Exercise

Look back over the last week. What were the most important tasks you had to do? If you succumbed to procrastination, jot down what unimportant tasks suddenly took priority. Now look ahead to next week. What are the most important tasks that you need to do? Jot down what plan you could make or tactics you might use to prevent procrastination happening again.

Organizing your time

Are you one of those people who would like an eight-, or even ten-, day week in which to get through everything? If so, you are not alone.

WHY DON'T WE MANAGE OUR TIME BETTER?

Actually, most of us don't manage our time at all – except in some vague sort of 'I'll try and find time for that on Sunday' way. We simply press on… and on… and on, until we feel swamped and our stress rates rise through the roof.

Here's a quiz to see how time-stressed you are:

How time-stressed are you?

In your Stress Journal rate each statement with a 0 (= never), 1 (= not often), 2 (= some of the time) or 3 (= all of the time). Add up your score at the end.

I feel that…

- ▶ I don't have enough time for leisure pursuits.
- ▶ I don't give my family the time I would like.
- ▶ I always feel 'behind' with chores and tasks.
- ▶ I cannot do my job well in the time that I have.
- ▶ I cannot say 'no' when people make time demands on me.
- ▶ I rarely ask others for help when overworked.
- ▶ I am often late for meetings and appointments.
- ▶ I get irritated with people who simply want to 'chat'.
- ▶ I rarely see my friends.
- ▶ No one seems to understand how busy I am.

Total:
0–10   You are in the 'normal' range.
10–20   You need to tighten up your time management.
20–30   You need to completely revamp your time management.

Here's how you can improve or revamp your time management.

For one week, keep a time log. It will look something like Table 6.1:

Table 6.1   Sample time log

Date: ....

Time	Activity	Time taken	Value of use of time
7.20 am	Lay awake in bed	20 mins	Could have got up sooner
8.00 a.m.	Rush to get ready for work	30 mins	Could have had more time if got up sooner
8.45 a.m.	Queue for cappuccino	10 mins	Kick-starts my day, so happy to give time to that
9.15 a.m.	Get rid of small tasks from list on desk	45 mins	Waste of time – could have delegated and spent time on project

Do you get the idea? Do this regularly for a week and you will begin to see how you can reorganize your day, cut out waste, and – who knows? – even find you have time for a little fun!

From now on, work with a weekly planner alongside a priorities list and put the important tasks in first. Once you have allowed adequate time for them, you can slot in unimportant tasks and social activities. There will be time for these with good time management – really!

Insight
▶ Managing time is vital when you feel stressed.
▶ It is your best resource – don't squander it.
▶ Stick as closely as you can to a written weekly plan for major tasks.

Setting your goals

Considering how simple and effective goal setting is, it is surprising that more of us don't use it as a regular tool. (Or perhaps you do. But do you achieve the goals you set?)

For most of us, even when we set goals, they often go awry.

Stop for a minute and ask yourself this question: 'Why?'

You may have come up with such thoughts as:

▶ 'My goals were unrealistic.'
▶ 'I set myself too many goals.'
▶ 'I found I didn't want my goals badly enough.'

GOAL-SETTING WEAKNESSES

One of the weaknesses of goal setting is if we make our goals too vague. If I say to you, 'I want to lose weight' (or you say that to me, perhaps), it actually means very little. I (or you) will probably not achieve it.

Insight
Goals that are vague are rarely achieved as they mean very little.

To really activate your goals:

▶ **Note them down:** Research has shown that those who note their goals down are much more likely to achieve them than those who say, 'My goals are in my head' – which tends to be where they stay!

- ▶ **Be specific:** Goals only become meaningful when they are SPECIFIC. In this instance, I would need to be able to tell you...
  - ▷ how much weight I want to lose
  - ▷ when I intend to lose it by (e.g. a friend's wedding day)
  - ▷ what type of diet I plan to go on
  - ▷ how I would manage eating out
  - ▷ how often I would go food shopping
  - ▷ and so on and so forth.

  Suddenly, the goal becomes real and achievable.
- ▶ **Break it down:** We fail with many of our goals simply because they are too big, too far away, too hard to achieve. We feel daunted and give up. Set small, easy goals that will build up to bigger targets as you go along.
- ▶ **Use a realistic time frame:** If we asked you to run a marathon with us and said it was next Monday, you would (probably!) turn it down. If we said it was next year, you might consider it. Why? Because the time frame is realistic. Don't be too ambitious with time frames. Give yourself space.

Here is another big word for goal setting: ACTION.

It really doesn't matter how many goal lists you make, or time limits you give them, or steps you break them down into, *unless you have an action plan*, nothing will happen. In Table 6.2, we give you an idea of what an action plan might look like. Use it – or one just like it.

Table 6.2   Sample action plan

GOAL	ACTION I am committed to take to achieve this goal (must be specific)
Ongoing (daily)	
Short-term (1 week – 1 month)	
Medium-term (1 month – 1 year)	
Long-term (over 1 year)	

Use your goal plan to work out your needs, and list the action you need to take *very specifically* in order to achieve them. For example, saying 'To lose weight' is too vague – you need to state how much, by when, and exactly how you plan to do it.

Exercise
Photocopy or otherwise reproduce our sample action plan (Table 6.2) and use it today to develop one goal that you have.

In future, use it to help you develop goals in general.

Clutter control

Clutter is an unusual stressor in that it is not especially 'active'. It is simply 'there'. Many people manage to...

▶ ignore it
▶ not mind it, *and*
▶ actively like it all around them.

However, for most people, a cluttered environment seems to jam up their brains as well and cause all kinds of stress and anxiety. For these people (you, perhaps?), clutter signifies...

▶ an inability to retain control
▶ a feeling of being overwhelmed
▶ fear that something really important may be buried in the morass
▶ the old 'What is wrong with me?' question that looms behind what seems like our complete inability to get our environment sorted out.

Most cluttered people do have a plan. You are probably one of these. You may have a list that has all your de-clutter projects written on it – 'Clean out garage', 'Take bags of old clothes to charity shop', 'Tidy all cupboards', 'Get large pile of office filing up to date.'

Accept that you are fooling yourself. Writing things down on bits of paper is not the same (at all) as actually doing it.

TOP EXCUSES FOR NOT DE-CLUTTERING

▶ 'It may come back into fashion.'
▶ 'I could need it again some day.'
▶ 'When I have time, I'll mend it.'
▶ 'One of the children might want it.'
▶ 'A messy desk makes me look busy.'
▶ 'When I retire I'll have time to read those.'
▶ 'I'm too busy with more important stuff.'
▶ 'I'll do a car boot sale / go onto eBay one day.'

…and so on!

The point about clutter is that, if you don't deal with it ruthlessly, it spreads. It is not static. It gets worse.

HERE'S HOW TO REDUCE IT

▶ **Set a semi-regular 'de-clutter' time:** You will not be able to give up every Sunday morning to this task, but decide on, say, two hours a week, and pick a day and time slot where you are usually free – 4 to 6 p.m. on a Saturday, for example.
▶ **Choose it or lose it:** This can be a hugely hard choice. First of all, remember – BE RUTHLESS! However, here is a get-out clause for the really agonizing choices. Have a 'pending tray'. This might be your garage, your garden shed, or your spare bedroom. Allow yourself a 'breather' before taking things to the tip. Bag them up in black bags / old storage boxes, and put them away – out of sight. You can then give yourself three months to get used to the idea that you have de-cluttered, and that you no longer need these things. *Then* go to the skip.
▶ **Call a charity or the Scouts or Guides:** Tell them that on such-and-such a date, you will have bag-loads of second-hand items that they may be able to sell or use. This commitment will be a great motivator, both from a time-frame point of view and a good-deed-done point of view.
▶ **Hire a skip:** Another time-frame motivator. Set aside a weekend in the future, and book the skip to arrive the day before. Skips cost good money these days, so you will want to stuff every tiny nook and cranny of the skip (remember to place mattresses, old pieces of wood and so on vertically to raise the height of the skip sides). Make a rule to undertake this 'skip weekend' annually.

▶ **Mementos:** Always a hard one, we appreciate. When just *looking* at old stuff brings back fond memories, it is hard to bin it. However, there are two possibilities here:

  1 *Keep a sample*: You don't need to keep every piece of hippy or punk clothing that you have collected – just one pair of flared pants or one black shirt will be just as evocative as a whole bundle of them.

  2 *Take a photo*: For example, keeping the children's old bikes or other toys clogs up space; a photo doesn't. Also, perhaps take a photo of the object along with its owner – start a small album of family members holding their old stuffed giraffe or whatever, and this will give you far more pleasure than having the actual things rotting away in the garage.

▶ Our last piece of advice is: GET STARTED. Take de-cluttering in stages, rather than try to achieve the impossible in a couple of hours. That way you will constantly feel you have achieved something, rather than failing again.

Insight
▶ Be ruthless.
▶ Set time boundaries.
▶ Get started – Rome wasn't built in a day, remember. Don't say that you won't start because you can't finish.

Exercise
Using the above suggestions, and any more ideas you have of your own, write down a De-Clutter Game Plan. Give yourself realistic timescales for this. Set yourself up to succeed, rather than simply placing more stress on yourself with impossible deadlines.

Then pick one small item – a kitchen drawer, for example – and tidy it up. How do you feel?

Prioritizing and delegating

Do you have a 'to do' list? If so, do you rate this list in order of priorities, as opposed to simply working through it? Perhaps not. This is partly because one way of feeling that we are keeping on top of tasks is by crossing as many of them off our 'to do' list as we can.

In order to achieve this, we stick with completing the quick-and-easy tasks. It makes the list look good, doesn't it? On the other hand, the longer, trickier, more important tasks don't get done.

You should prioritize your 'to do' list into the following categories:

- ▶ Important and urgent: high priority
- ▶ Important but not urgent: medium priority
- ▶ Urgent but not important: low priority
- ▶ Neither urgent nor important: don't waste your time!

DELEGATING

Most of us under pressure do this far too little. Underneath this reluctance often lurks the old maxim, 'I can do it better/quicker myself.' Often, this is quite true – at least, to begin with. But if you do the same thing ten times, that's a lot of time. Take a couple of times to go slower as you show someone else how to do it, and you won't need to do it at all the other eight times.

'I know, I know. But…' Yes, we understand – no one quite grasps the problem the way you do, no one will be as conscientious about it as you are and when you've delegated in the past, people have made a mess of things…

So here's how to delegate:

- ▶ Do it genuinely. Don't hover in the background watching and worrying. That will be more stressful than ever (for both of you).
- ▶ Select someone you trust to get the job at least half right. You can teach them the rest.
- ▶ Even if the job isn't quite up to scratch, ask yourself, 'Does that really matter?' You are probably delegating less important tasks in any event.
- ▶ Be very appreciative. Praise what they have done well – you want them to help you more often, not less, in the future.
- ▶ If you really cannot get help from below, get it from above. Ask your line manager to recommend someone who might like to learn or have some spare time. They will be more aware of any 'slack' in the bigger picture.
- ▶ Use the same skills at home with your family. Children love to help and it is excellent for development of responsibility. If it's not as good as you would have done, don't worry. The rewards of delegating to children are huge.

Organizing your paperwork

'Clutter' – which we have discussed already – to many people means 'paperwork'. Even in these days of electronic communications and 'paper-free offices', for most of us the barrage of paperwork that drops onto our doormat seems relentless and unstoppable.

Most of us flounder in a sea of paperwork because we do not act instantly. Advertisers are very cunning. They don't want you to bin their unsolicited mail; of course they don't. So they try every trick in the book to get you to look at it and hang on to it.

The old 'I might need to know about that / use that / buy one of those one day' thought is what keeps paper piling up around us. Do you rip articles out of magazines with alluring titles such as '50 ways to look thinner', 'How to banish greenfly', 'Sell your second-hand car for more than you paid for it', etc.? You are not alone. However…

STOP IT!

▶ Keep a small basket in a corner of your hallway and immediately put all junk mail in it.
▶ Open all other mail straight away and bin anything that does not need a response.
▶ Charity requests: hard just to ditch them, so collect them in a box, and once every few weeks or months (depending on your bank balance) get one of your children to 'lucky dip' one out of the box, and send a small sum to that particular charity. Bin the rest and start again.

- Have an efficient filing system. A good idea is to do your filing only once every, say, three months. Store it in a tray or box until then. When you come to do it, you will find that 50 per cent of the paperwork you thought, three months ago, needed keeping can actually be thrown away. Just file the important things that are left.
- Don't have too many files. Keeping a file labelled 'Hernia operation possibilities' is too specific (unless you are about to have a hernia operation). Just have one 'Health advice, general' file (if you must keep stuff like this).
- Keep a small, fireproof, safety deposit box for vital papers such as birth certificates, house deeds, your will, share certificates and passports. Then you will always know where the really important things are – as will your family, in an emergency.
- Keep a large wicker basket next to your waste bin in your kitchen/utility area. Throw all papers and magazines into it as soon as they are read. This saves them from cluttering up coffee tables, but you will still have access to them for a few days if you recall something urgent that you wanted to look at.

Insight

Paperwork can multiply quickly and become difficult to discard if not dealt with IMMEDIATELY.

Keeping up the good work

Staying organized may be as difficult as *getting* organized. Don't run the risk of simply sinking back into disorganization by becoming passive. Make a list of all the things that work for you, and that you intend to keep on doing. Think less in terms of how to organize your complex life so that it works a little better, and more in terms of how to simplify your life through organization, so that you have more time, a tidier environment and clearer goals.

KEEP IN MIND

1 Keep your goals in the forefront of your mind. How? You know the answer by now – WRITE THEM DOWN. Check that your short-term goals are in line with those you have set for the medium and long term. If you encounter any hiccups, you can adjust your goals accordingly. They are not cast in concrete, but you need to be working towards them all the time.

2 Don't just have a 'to do' list, prioritize it.

3 Keep track of time-wasting and procrastination. You know when you are doing it, so CUT IT OUT! You will be better served by building in longer time periods for achieving the important tasks in your life, and using any extra time you have to 'reward' yourself with something purely pleasurable. This way, you still enjoy 'time out' but don't suffer the stress that goes with time-wasting.

4 You must learn to say 'no' and to delegate. If you want to turn into a frazzled wreck, be our guest, but that will be (if it is not already) the result of a) not being firm and b) not accepting that others can do things (maybe not quite as well as you, but close enough).

5 If you delegate, then be very appreciative. Praise what the person you have delegated to has done well – you want them to help you more often, not less, in the future.

6 Stop giving yourself and others excuses for not de-cluttering.

7 Ensure that you live and work in an environment that doesn't stress you out because it is messy, noisy or irritating to you in any other way. Work at keeping it the way you want it. BE RUTHLESS WITH CLUTTER.

8 Do two tasks at once where you can. For example, you can toast your bread while talking on the phone, or pedal an exercise bike while watching TV.

9 Invest in good storage.

7

Overcoming stress-related anger

In this chapter you will learn:
- *whether stress is raising your anger levels*
- *that anger isn't always a bad thing – it is how you use it that matters*
- *some tools for reducing angry thoughts and feelings*
- *who is responsible for your anger, and why*
- *that humour is a great de-stressor.*

How stress causes anger

How much of your stress do you think is caused by the fact that you get angry quite quickly and easily? How much of your anger do you think is caused by stress?

Whichever way you look at it, if you find yourself getting angry quite quickly, a lot of the time, you have a problem and need to deal with it. Not only is anger very stressful, it can ruin both personal and professional relationships, as well as be detrimental to your health.

ANGER CAN ALSO KILL

Road rage is an example. An otherwise rational man or woman, after getting 'cut up' by another driver, becomes so angry that he/she decides to get his/her own back by giving chase. An accident results that kills both drivers. Stress in general may have provoked this crazy, destructive behaviour. Too much to do, setting off late, not allowing enough time to get from A to B, generally feeling that people are inconsiderate – stressors such as these close the gap between rational thinking and angry thinking.

TWENTY-FIRST-CENTURY INTOLERANCE

We are more concerned than ever with 'our rights' (fuelled, very often, by our compensation culture). We are less philosophical, less inclined to 'put things down to experience'. If our demands are not now met in a way that we have come to expect, we become angry.

OTHERS GET ANGRIER AS WELL

As we become generally angrier – so do others. This means it takes a lot less for us to get into a fight with someone, or to be provoked ourselves.

SUPPRESSING ANGER

Unfortunately, especially in the workplace, expressing anger is becoming less and less acceptable. This means that by expressing anger inappropriately we may risk our job, or at least disciplinary action. We might be sued by someone who feels that we have exhibited aggression towards them. We therefore often bottle anger up, instead of dealing with it, and this can be exceedingly harmful to both our emotional and physical wellbeing.

Me? Angry?

One difficulty can be anger self-assessment. What may seem an angry response to person A is a natural way of dealing with situations to person B.

Are you aware of your own anger? Do the following questionnaire:

Questionnaire: How aware of your anger are you?

Rate the following statements to check out your anger awareness: 0 = never, 1 = occasionally, 2 = often. Add up your answers.

- ▶ Others comment on my aggressive responses.
- ▶ Waiting in queues drives me mad.
- ▶ I can't tolerate rudeness.
- ▶ I always respond badly to criticism.
- ▶ I start arguments easily.

- ▶ Driving in traffic causes me huge stress.
- ▶ I consider most other drivers on the road to be bad drivers.
- ▶ I find most shop assistants, helplines, etc., quite incompetent.
- ▶ In difficult discussions with people, I tend to get the angriest most quickly.
- ▶ I let petty annoyances really work me up.

Scores:

- ▶ 0–7   Don't worry – you stay well balanced in most tricky situations.
- ▶ 8–14   You are responding to stressful situations with anger too often.
- ▶ 15–20   Your angry responses may cause some serious damage if you don't make urgent changes.

Insight

- ▶ Stress can cause us to become angry quite easily.
- ▶ Anger can damage our emotional and physical health, as well as ruining relationships and possibly costing us our jobs.
- ▶ Accepting that we do get inappropriately angry is half the battle in reducing such responses.

When anger can be healthy

What would you say are the differences between healthy, constructive anger and unhealthy, destructive anger? Any ideas?

Have you ever thought of anger as being a good thing? If not, consider for a moment, and write down three or four suggestions as to when this might be the case.

Let's take a look at some possibilities:

- ▶ **Anger at injustice:** You see someone kicking a dog, hear on the news that innocent people in a far-off country are being brutally treated, notice someone at work who is always unfairly picked on by the boss... These are situations where injustice prevails, and we need to get angry about these things. World starvation, unnecessary wars, people dying through lack of healthcare – the only way to get anything done about such situations is for at least some of us to feel angry about them.

- ▶ **Anger to get results:** As a last resort (we stress), if you really need to get results from recalcitrant staff, motor mechanics, waiters, your children, etc., then reasonable anger can work a treat.
- ▶ **Anger as a motivational tool:** When you finally hear yourself (or someone else) say, 'Right. That's it. I'm not taking any more of this…' you know that either you (or they) are going to blow their top in order to get some action. In a sense, you are bringing some energy to the situation.
- ▶ **Anger as a release:** 'Letting it all out' has actually been shown to have health benefits, compared to repressed anger, which we hold inside and which eats away at us. However, there are ways of letting things out that don't involve us becoming apoplectic, so use this with caution.
- ▶ **Anger as an alert signal:** Healthy anger can be letting you know that something is wrong. You can use this alert to figure out what is worrying you, and then do something positive to change it. For example, if you find yourself becoming irritated every time you need to meet with a particular work colleague, ask yourself why they annoy you so. It may be that they are always late for your meetings, always dominate the discussion, regularly cancel at the last minute, and so on. Becoming aware of your anger in these circumstances encourages you to change the situation so that it is less stressful.

Insight

Don't attempt to eliminate anger from your life – there are many ways in which healthy anger can be a helpful and motivating tool.

Exercise

Jot down two or three situations in which you became angry in the last week or two. Now think for a moment about the outcomes. Do you feel that, in any of these instances, the anger achieved a good result? Does this help you to see that anger can actually be healthy?

The anger spiral

Anger is built on our expectations regarding the ideals and behaviours of others. We expect people to treat us fairly and sometimes they don't. We expect them to be nice to us and sometimes they aren't. We expect them to help us and sometimes they walk away.

Each time someone breaks a rule of ours, violates a contract or acts against our wishes, a possible option is to react with anger. We do not absolutely have to – it is our choice. Unfortunately, we do not always feel that we are in control of this choice – it is as though it has already been decided for us, and we act accordingly.

Earlier in this book we worked with you on learning to challenge your thinking. We need you now to use the skills you have learned to help you to reduce your angry thoughts and feelings.

You understand well now the relationship between what we think and how we feel. A situation such as a rude boss may be the external trigger and our thought 'My boss should not be rude to me' triggers the emotion of anger. It is the thought that drives the emotion – at least initially. However, once in the spiral, the emotion then drives further negative thoughts, such as 'He really is a bully. He shouldn't be allowed to get away with it.' In turn, this makes you angrier than before – and so on, until the anger gets quite out of control.

This may sound all too familiar to you.

However, help is at hand. In this chapter we will show you a variety of 'Get out of Jail Free' cards that can take you out of the anger spiral and back into the stress-free zone.

Insight
▶ We make ourselves angry when our expectations of how others should behave are not met.
▶ This can lead us into an anger spiral that escalates the angry feelings that we have and makes situations worse.

Exercise
Have you recently found yourself in an anger spiral? Jot down how you felt (from mildly irritated to fuming) at the start of the situation, the middle of the situation and the end of the situation. Did your anger increase in the way we have described above as your thinking became more negative about the situation? How long did it take for your anger to subside?

Getting out of the anger spiral

Let's take a look at someone who gets into an anger spiral – and learn from his mistake. We'll use thought challenging as our tool to see how we can help our guinea pig reduce his angry thoughts and responses.

Peter is a 35-year-old computer specialist. He works in a high-pressure job, feels stressed most of the time, and is perpetually offended at a myriad of slights and abuses. He is highly competitive and takes absolutely nothing lightly. In his mind, others are just out to annoy him, make his life difficult, and increase his stress – an indifferent shop assistant, a slow driver ahead of him, a leisurely bank clerk – any of these things can trigger his rage.

Is Peter similar to you? Do you find yourself reacting in a similar way, at least on occasions when you feel especially stressed?

To help Peter, we're going to break his pattern of anger down into a series of steps. Each step represents a 'choice point'. He can choose to intervene at each step, cool down and break the pattern – or he can continue down his destructive path. (But don't let the latter happen to you.)

> **Exercise**
> Get ahead of the game. See if you can work out ahead of time what Peter could do to get out of his anger spiral. Then check your thinking with what happens.

Below we'll look at the six main ways or steps Peter could take to break his anger spiral:

1 BREAKING THE 'SHOULD' RULE

The most important step consists of breaking the 'should' rule. Much of Peter's life is governed by such rules. He has rules and expectations for his own behaviour, for others' behaviour, and even feels the weight of others' rules on him. He has more rules than a legal tome. The result? Anger, guilt, and intense pressure to live up to his standards.

But he cannot live up to such unrelenting standards, and neither can others (and neither can you). Peter demands, 'People should listen to me', 'They should stay out of the way', 'I should have total control over this situation.' But the fact of the matter is that people don't listen, they do get in his way, and he cannot control their behaviour. At this point, Peter has the choice to accept the circumstances that have arisen or hammer away against reality, demanding that it should not be that way.

Of course, it would be very much preferable if he was listened to and left alone, but he cannot *demand* it.

Peter now has an option to challenge the 'should' style of thinking that is causing him to get so angry. What else could Peter say instead of the thoughts above? Cover the rest of this page and write a short script for Peter. Then take a look and see if you were thinking along the right lines.

Here is our suggestion:

> *'The fact of the matter is that people do ignore my wishes and intrude. What, constructively, can I do when that happens? I can continue to follow my own 'rules', to treat others fairly and well, but not to insist that they respond to me in the same way. It would be nice if they did, but if they don't, they don't. I need to stop disturbing myself about something I can do nothing about.'*

Insight
▶ Rigid thinking, with lots of 'shoulds' in it, will ensure that we get high blood pressure very quickly when others fail to respond to our rules.
▶ Learning to be more flexible in our views of how others behave will reduce anger and stress.

Coming to terms with the idea that others might very well not follow our own ideas about behaviour is a good start. Let's, however, look at some other steps we can take that can help to calm the situation down...

2 WORK OUT WHAT'S REALLY UPSETTING YOU

Another step we could take to get out of the anger spiral is to examine what really hurts us when one of our rules is broken. For example, when Peter is angry and hurt, he can ask himself: 'What really hurts here?' Maybe he thinks: 'People are rude and insensitive',

'I'll be made the victim', or 'I'm powerless to do anything about this.' What hurts the most is Peter's inability to change people's behaviour.

What could he tell himself instead of having the thoughts above? Cover the rest of the page and write a short script for Peter. Then check your ideas against ours.

Here is our suggestion:

> *'There is no evidence that I should be able to control people. They are responsible for their own beliefs, behaviours, attitudes and assumptions. Perhaps I can see myself not as a victim, but as a person who can choose how to be.'*

3 KEEP YOUR COOL

The third step we could take is to respond to hot, anger-driven thoughts with cooler, more level-headed ones. Peter initially thinks, 'How dare he?', but he could replace that thought with 'He thinks he is trying to help me.' Peter thinks, 'How stupid can she be?', but he could instead respond, 'She's human.'

Are you getting the idea?

Insight
To reduce your anger, change your script.

Exercise
Who or what annoyed you the most in the last couple of days? Write down the situation, rate how angry you felt (1–10) and what you were thinking.

Using any of the three tools we've come up with so far – change the script. How angry do you think these alternative thoughts would make you (1–10)?

4 USE RELAXATION SKILLS

The next step is to respond to the angry feelings themselves. Peter can do this by practising relaxation and deep breathing. He can relax his muscles, and refocus his attention away from the stressful situation.

The relaxation and breathing skills you have hopefully mastered should now come into their own.

5 PREVENT STRESS AND ANGER FROM MAKING US SPITEFUL

The fifth step is for Peter to look at how, by his angry thinking, he gives himself permission to think in a thoroughly spiteful way. These thoughts allow Peter to treat others in ways that he himself would not want to be treated: 'He deserved it.' 'I just want her to hurt the way I have been hurt.' 'This is the only way I can get my point across.' (have you ever had any thoughts along these lines?) Peter can recognize these ideas as 'con artistry'. They con him into throwing aside his morals and engaging in threats, sarcasm and demands.

Peter needs to remind himself of the costs of such strategies, and the benefits of remaining calm and fair.

6 GET CONTROL OF AGGRESSIVE BEHAVIOUR

The sixth step is to look at the aggressive behaviour that comes from angry thinking. Peter gives himself permission to act aggressively and ignore the rights of other people. Imagine Peter getting worked up with a sales assistant who is interminably slow. He starts speaking loudly and rudely, and demanding to see the manager. The assistant then gets angry back and a row ensues.

What other choices does Peter have?

▶ He could attempt to understand the cause of the assistant's slowness.
▶ He can put himself in the other person's shoes, imagine what he is thinking and feeling, and attempt to understand his point of view.
▶ He can ask himself how important this delay really is.

This will help to...

1 decrease Peter's anger
2 decrease the other man's anger
3 increase the likelihood that the other man will hear what Peter has to say
4 increase the likelihood of the two of them having a rational and reasonable conversation.

- ▶ Keep up with your deep breathing and relaxation practice to help you when you feel your anger rising.
- ▶ Don't give yourself permission to think spiteful thoughts.
- ▶ Don't let aggressive behaviour control you.

Learning to own your own anger

One of the difficulties we can have in keeping calm in provocative situations is the idea that none of this is our fault. If the other person had not done this, that or the other, we would never have reacted in that way. Therefore, it *was* their fault, wasn't it?

Actually, you may be partially right. Someone may well have been extremely thoughtless, careless, acted stupidly or whatever, and you may well be the victim of their rotten judgement. However, while the other person is responsible for their actions...

YOU ARE RESPONSIBLE FOR YOUR RESPONSE.

Let's look at an example:

Sally had been having a terrible day. Things were going badly at work and she was under a lot of stress. She had social plans for the evening, but the work tasks kept rolling onto her desk, and they were all marked 'urgent'. Finally, Sally felt that she had things under enough control to shut down her computer and head for the door.

Looking at her watch, Sally saw that she had just enough time to make her engagement and not be late, provided she had a good journey home, and no hold-ups. Sally walked quickly to her car, where she noticed, to her absolute horror, that a delivery truck was parked right across her bay, blocking her in. Sally just could not believe it. She felt anger rise up within her. Her heart started beating fast and a hot rush of emotion welled up inside her.

Looking round, she saw the probable driver of the vehicle standing chatting with someone further up the car park. This added to Sally's anger. 'How dare he!' she thought. 'Not only has he blocked my space, but he is in no hurry to do anything about it.' Sally rushed up to the man and started shouting at him.

'You selfish idiot! Can't you see you have blocked me in. I'm going to miss a theatre date because of your selfishness.'

'Keep your hair on' was the response Sally got. 'No need to get so uptight about it. I'll be there in a minute.'

Sally went through the roof! This was so unjust, so unfair, and she simply 'lost it' at the outrageous way she perceived the driver to be behaving. She starting screaming at him at the top of her voice, and even swung her briefcase towards the man, hitting him on the leg. He moved to defend himself and a bystander had to restrain Sally, who ended up so distraught she had to be taken back to her office reception area to calm down.

Needless to say, she never made the theatre.

Who do you consider was to blame for Sally's anger and distress?

- ▶ Hands up if you thought the lorry driver.
- ▶ Hands up if you thought his friend contributed.
- ▶ Hands up if you think the overall unfortunate circumstances were the problem.
- ▶ Hands up if you think that Sally was the culprit.

When we tell you that the answer is Sally, by 100 per cent, what do you think about that? (Hands up if you think we're wrong.)

Let's look at the scenario again.

The truck driver was to blame for:

- ▶ thoughtless parking
- ▶ time-wasting when he should have been delivering his goods
- ▶ total insensitivity to Sally's predicament
- ▶ his rude response when she pointed it out to him.

What was Sally to blame for?

- ▶ Allowing herself to become so angry that she lost control of the situation.

Defusing stress with humour

You finally decide on the new bookcase you want for your lounge. Seeing that it is much cheaper to build it yourself, you purchase the 'flat-pack' version. However, when you get it home, you discover that the instructions were written by someone for whom English was definitely not their first language, and that all the nuts and bolts look the same. It takes you the best part of a day to put up – despite the words 'easy to assemble' being printed all over the packaging – and when you start to place your books on the shelves, the whole thing falls apart.

QUESTION 1

How do you react? Do you...

▶ fume?
▶ cry?
▶ have a laugh?

Be totally honest about this. We suspect that, if you are, most of you will have admitted to the first or second options.

QUESTION 2

What difference to the final outcome do any of these responses make?

Answer: Zero.

QUESTION 3

With this in mind, which of the above responses is likely to relieve your stress the most?

Answer: Almost certainly, laughing.

We do appreciate that you might think it's not at all funny and very frustrating ('I spent all day... etc.' – all understood). However, here's yet another question: If someone else told you this story in the pub or at a supper party, how would you respond?

Answer: We suspect you'd laugh.

So what do you make of all this? Is your response one of these?

▶ 'It's funny when it happens to someone else, but not when it happens to me.'
▶ 'It's hard to see the funny side of such things at the time.'
▶ 'I don't actively look for the funny side of things.'
▶ 'It's childish to use humour when something goes wrong.'

Or, just possibly...

▶ 'Perhaps I need to cultivate using humour more as an alternative to getting worked up, angry and stressed out.'

In case this might be something you would benefit from learning about, we will now look at the many benefits of using humour – and how to make it your first option, rather than a last resort.

Insight
Seeing the funny side of things is less stressful than getting angry.

Exercise
When did you last laugh at yourself? What happened? Now look through your notes to one or two stressful situations you have recorded. Rethink the situation – could you have used humour? If you told the tale to a friend at a later stage, would it have sounded humorous to them?

Look back over the last two weeks. Write down the situations that stressed you out the most (three or four of them, if you can). Now, just supposing you were asked to see a funny side to what happened, or to your reaction to what happened, could you? Write your suggestions down.

Laugh to improve your health

Almost all of us feel better when we have a laugh. However, you may not be aware of quite what a good stress-buster laughter is – which is why we are spending some time and effort on it in this book.

Can you think of any ways that laughing might actually help you physically? Cover the rest of this page, and then jot them down.

Here are some good ways that humour can lower stress. Did you come up with any yourself? Top marks if you did.

▶ You relax.
▶ Humour stops you getting even more worked up.
▶ You now understand the anger spiral – stress begets stress, and on it goes, until we explode or implode. So, even if you start off by getting distressed (that bookcase falling down was quite a dreadful thing to happen!), you can stop the spiral going ever upward by 'breaking' the situation with humour.
▶ You strengthen your immune system. More laughter equals less stress, equals less harmful stress hormones circulating round your body. That must be good.
▶ Laughter is infectious and habit-forming. 'Practising laughing' is no different to practising anything else. The more you do it, the easier and more quickly it will become a natural 'first resort'. So even though it might not be your normal first response, try to begin to look for the funny side of things.
▶ Laughing at ourselves stops us winding ourselves up. Remember how we looked at the way stress increases according to the importance we give to a situation going wrong? Well, this is just the same with us. Often, we take ourselves too seriously – we look for perfection and get stressed when we fail to achieve it. Learn to laugh at your errors and cock-ups instead. Not only will you see that things matter a lot less than you thought – you will give others the chance to share a joke as well.
▶ Laughter is very good for you physically as well as emotionally. Learn to 'practise' seeing the funny side of things, so that it becomes more natural to do so.

Making humour your first option, not your last resort

HOW CAN I 'PRACTISE' LAUGHING?

This – as we have already said – is no different to practising anything else. Begin by writing down situations where everything has gone wrong. Then ask yourself two questions:

1 Was there anything at all humorous in this situation? For example, you have spent the day deliberately trying not to hear the football results before you get to watch *Match of the Day*, only to have your eight-year-old son tell the result to you just as you sit down to watch it. You could go through the roof, or sigh with despair. However, it is also quite a funny story (honestly).

2 Could I perhaps have looked at things more light-heartedly? For example, you are running desperately to catch a bus, knowing that if you miss it you will have to wait half an hour for the next one. As you reach it, you slip, your scarf gets caught on a hedge and starts strangling you, and when you reach out to steady yourself, you grab someone else who falls over with you. No one is hurt, and the person you pull over is smiling at the ridiculous train of events – but you don't catch the bus. Is this a funny story or a horror story? If you see it as a funny story – and more importantly, did so at the time that it happened – your stress levels will be a lot lower.

An extra suggestion – watch more stand-up comedians live or on TV.

Yes, really. These people make the most dire situations sound hilarious, and the more you listen, the more you will learn how to do the same. So 'get out there' and start practising.

We are not suggesting that *all* situations can boast a humorous side, and we appreciate that many don't.

Here are two specific instances when laughter is NOT the right response:

1 **Inappropriate laughter:** This usually involves not laughing at other people's misfortunes, not laughing when a mess-up has

caused a serious or harmful result, and not laughing when it is obvious that everyone else is taking whatever-it-is very seriously. Hopefully, your instincts will tell you when laughter is inappropriate. If not, then spend some time learning to apologize well.

2 **Malicious laughter:** We hope you will know exactly what we mean here. If you had either red hair or glasses at school, you will understand entirely how horrendous malicious laughter is. Poking fun at others to raise a laugh, telling stories that show others up in a poor light, hooting when someone spills burning coffee on themselves – these are not ways to make friends, or even to reduce your stress levels. Only use this type of laughter on yourself.

Insight

▶ Find the humorous side of a situation as a first, rather than a last, resort.

▶ Laughter isn't always appropriate – use discretion.

Exercise
Take a piece of paper and draw a line down the middle of the page. On one side, write down the latest stressful incident, and on the other side, write down any comic elements (look back at the previous examples if you are struggling). Continue to do this at least twice a week for two months – or until it becomes more natural for you to see the funny side of things more easily.

Some final points on anger

You are now becoming an expert at managing anger. However, before we move on, here are just a few more points that we believe will assist you:

'LETTING IT ALL OUT' – ISN'T THIS HEALTHIER THAN KEEPING IT BOTTLED UP?

Well, yes and no. Think about people you know who constantly vent their anger. Don't they simply seem angry all the time? Aren't they the sort of people you avoid confrontations with if you can?

Releasing your anger can actually become just as much of a habit as anything else. You will get used to exploding, and react instinctively in a hostile way. 'Letting it all out' is not going to reduce your anger habit at all.

Equally, neither is bottling it up. Fuming internally while saying nothing is not at all healthy. Such unhelpful strategies are likely to increase your blood pressure. The key is to 'repackage' what you want to express in a healthier and less confrontational way.

STRATEGIES FOR KEEPING CALM

This is a variation on the work we have done in previous chapters on challenging negative or unhelpful thoughts. When you feel yourself getting worked up, instead of feeding the anger by saying to yourself, for example, 'That guy's an idiot' or 'This queue is never going to move', use calming self-suggestions instead. A few examples might be:

- ▶ 'Is this really worth getting worked up about?'
- ▶ 'Does getting angry help the situation?'
- ▶ 'Other people can do what they wish.'
- ▶ 'I'm not going to take this personally.'
- ▶ 'I don't *have* to get angry. It's my choice.'
- ▶ 'The guy is fallible just like the rest of us.'
- ▶ 'I'm living proof that I can stand queuing.'
- ▶ 'I'll take some deep breaths and stay calm.'

We'd like you to think up some calming thoughts of your own as you will know what works for you better than we do. The important strategy is to find a self-statement to say to yourself that will reduce your anger rather than increase it.

REHEARSING SITUATIONS THAT YOU HAVE BECOME ANGRY ABOUT IN THE PAST

Sometimes, we find ourselves getting wound up again and again by the same old stuff. How futile is this? So, if you know a situation is coming up that normally irritates you – for example, the meaningless team meetings you have to sit through every Monday – rehearse ahead of time what you can do to reduce or eliminate this annoyance, rather than simply accepting it as a fact of life.

WAITING TO GET ANGRY – COUNTING TO TEN

An old adage, but it can often work. 'Count to ten' might mean leaving the situation for a while, distracting yourself for a time and returning to your angry thoughts after a break, to see if they have reduced, or it might literally mean just that – counting inside your head. In any event, pausing mentally before 'going in' can be a helpful way of calming down.

Insight
▶ Venting anger is not a good idea. Learn to repackage your messages in a less hostile way.
▶ Have a stock of calming statements to defuse angry thinking.
▶ Don't keep getting angry about the same old things.
▶ Count to ten!

Exercise
Write down the heading 'Calming self-talk for angry situations' on a sheet of paper or in a word-processing document and note down at least six sentences that you feel would work for you. Add to this list regularly, so that you build up a good stock of helpful challenges to your angry thoughts.

KEEP IN MIND

1 Not only is anger stressful for you, it can spoil relationships and be detrimental to your health. So dealing with it is a necessity.

2 As we get angrier, so do others, which means we get into fights and arguments more easily when others provoke us.

3 Anger is not always a bad thing. Anger at injustice, for example, is essential to prevent bad things happening. In essence, there is appropriate anger and inappropriate anger – inappropriate anger is what is so bad for us.

4 As long as we retain the idea that others make us angry, it is hard to change. Grasp the fundamental truth that we are the ones who decide to get angry or not and we always have a choice.

5 You may have a 'should' rule about how life should go or how others should behave and you get angry when this is violated. Take the option to challenge your 'should' rule and replace it with more open-minded views. Your anger will reduce instantly.

6 Coming to terms with the idea that others may not follow or share your ideas and views can be extremely difficult if your beliefs are strong. Learning to be more flexible in your views will take time but will become easier if you remember that your and other people's thinking is usually no more than a point of view, and we are all entitled to that. What we are not entitled to is to insist that others see things as we do.

7 Don't waste your time and energy going over situations that you have become angry about in the past.

8 Relaxation skills that you have already learned about in Chapter 5 are exceedingly helpful in defusing angry thoughts.

9 Use humour to defuse anger. Attempt to see the 'funny side', as this is more likely to reduce stress than an angry outburst.

10 Keep in your mind the strategies for keeping calm referred to in this chapter. Venting your anger is rarely a good idea as it prevents people from actually hearing the message you want to convey. All they note is the angry outburst and your (possibly very good) point is missed.

'It's not me, it's everybody else!' – de-stress by improving your communication skills

In this chapter you will learn:
- *that it is easier to deal with difficult people and situations if we improve our own communication skills*
- *the importance of listening*
- *the strengths of assertive behaviour in helping you to communicate well and achieve your goals*
- *skills to prevent others manipulating you*
- *how to defuse abusive behaviour from others.*

Why communicate?

Do you ever feel that it is really not you, but everybody else, who is difficult, rude and obstructive, and adds to (or is even the sole cause of) most of the stress in your life? These others may be your family, they may be your work colleagues, they may simply be irritating 'types' – those, for example, who chat away to shop assistants, unaware that the queue behind them grows longer and longer as they do so.

You are not alone!

However, as you have already learned, it is a hard task to change the attitudes and behaviours of others – all we can try to do is to influence them. Getting stressed about it is even more exhausting. Learning to improve your own communication skills is a positive way forward. We can anticipate some of your responses to this:

- ▶ 'Why should I?'
- ▶ 'Why do I need to be the one to make the big effort?'
- ▶ 'Let them learn to communicate better with me.'

All good points. However, they get you no further forward and 'getting further forward' equals becoming less stressed – and this is the important thing.

Think about the reasons we need to communicate…

- ▶ to pass on information
- ▶ to ask for what we want
- ▶ to share how we feel
- ▶ to understand how others feel
- ▶ to achieve goals and outcomes.

Insight

If we learn to communicate well, we are more likely to get what we want. This is a huge benefit of communicating well. In addition, we are more likely to command the respect of others, and we are usually happier about ourselves (equals more relaxed, equals less stressed).

A key feature of communicating well is to ensure that people understand the point we are making. Too often, we simply assume that they do, which can be a mistake. Here are some wonderful examples, from a variety of locations, of the communication errors people can make:

AFTER MAKING TEA, STAFF SHOULD EMPTY TEAPOT AND STAND UPSIDE DOWN ON DRAINING BOARD.

WOULD THE PERSON WHO TOOK THE STEP LADDER PLEASE RETURN IT IMMEDIATELY OR FURTHER STEPS WILL BE TAKEN.

AUTOMATIC WASHING MACHINES: PLEASE REMOVE ALL YOUR CLOTHES WHEN RED LIGHT GOES OUT.

TOILET OUT OF ORDER: PLEASE USE FLOOR BELOW.

Insight

While we may feel that other people wind us up, improving our own communication skills can get us closer to the results we want.

Shhh! What can you hear?

Communication is not just about talking. It is about listening and understanding.

One reason for failing to relate well to others is that we become very self-focused in conversations. We are often either 'talking or waiting'. In other words, when we are not speaking ourselves, we are simply preparing for the next opportunity to speak, rather than actively listening to the other person, and showing them that we understand what they are saying.

LISTENING SKILLS

Listening skills are very important. Develop them if you are a poor listener. Otherwise, people won't relate to you well, and your personal and work relationships will almost certainly not be as good as they could be. Good listeners tend to have less stress in their lives, as they quite simply get on better with people.

CHOOSE THE RIGHT TIME

In order to be a good listener, you will benefit from being in the right frame of mind. You also need to be sure that this is a good time for the person who needs to speak to you. Do they want to talk to you now? Would later be better? Become aware of your own needs and feelings. Will you focus better when you have made that urgent phone call?

It is important to be able to give others the time they need to express themselves, so timing can be crucially important.

BE AN ACTIVE LISTENER

We have all experienced, at some point or another, telling somebody something important and getting little or no response. This didn't necessarily mean that they were not listening – but it might have done. Being active in your listening involves indicating to the other person that you are focusing on what they have to say. You can do this by:

▶ saying 'I see', 'I understand', 'Go on', etc. – short phrases that indicate that you are 'with' the other person
▶ using facial expressions to reflect what is being said – a smile, a frown, a nod, etc., are all powerful indicators that you are listening closely.

If you are not certain what exactly has been said, say so: 'I'm not sure what you mean by that.' 'When did this happen exactly?', 'Were you angry or disappointed?' Ask whatever questions you need to ensure that you completely understand the situation.

ACKNOWLEDGE UNDERSTANDING WITH FEEDBACK

We usually feel most listened to and understood when someone reflects back to us what we have just said. While this may not sound an excessively clever thing to do, it is extraordinarily powerful.

> *'It sounds as though you are really struggling at present. Tom's away a great deal and, with three children under five, it is often too much to cope with on your own.'*

The relief of being able to say, 'Yes, that's exactly how it is,' and knowing that you have been listened to and understood, creates great respect and closeness between two people.

UNDERSTANDING IS ENABLING

A further important advantage of truly understanding the other person's point of view is that they will (almost certainly) be far more receptive to hearing yours in due course, with the possibility of a constructive result as the outcome.

Insight
▶ Communicating well involves listening and understanding as well as talking.
▶ Listening improves our relationships with others, which means they are likely to be more harmonious and less stressful.

Your turn to talk – what is your personal style?

What you say, and how you say it, will decide whether you achieve a good (and possibly harmonious) outcome, or feel more stressed than ever when the conversation ends.

What is your personal style?

Do you tend to be:

- ▶ passive ('Oh, all right then.')
- ▶ aggressive ('Because I say so, that's why.')
- ▶ assertive ('I'd like to help, but I'm too busy right now.')

Look at these examples:

Jane and Simon go to Simon's office party together. However, soon after they arrive, Simon drifts off and starts chatting to people that Jane does not know. He does not introduce her, but leaves her to her own devices. Jane does not like to interrupt, but when she sees Simon go off on his own to get a drink, she goes up to him and tells him how isolated she feels. As she does so, she starts to cry. Simon tells her not to be so silly, that it is work and that he won't be long. Jane accepts this meekly and sits in a chair on her own for a further hour before Simon is willing to leave.

Tom comes home after a tiring day at work, looking forward to a quiet drink to unwind before dinner. His wife Gina has other ideas. She wants to tell Tom how difficult the children have been, how the lawn mower broke down, and what a mess he left the bathroom in this morning. Tom refuses to listen, and Gina explodes and tells Tom that either he listens to her now or packs his bags. Tom does listen then, but feels resentful that he isn't being given time to relax.

Lisa's boss asks her to stay late to work on a night that she has theatre tickets. When she tells him this, he says, 'But this is vital. It is for a meeting at 9 a.m. tomorrow for a most important client.' Jane responds, 'I'm really sorry. I appreciate how important it is, but I cannot stay late tonight. If it helps, I would be happy to come in early tomorrow morning, to ensure that you have the work before 9 a.m.' Her boss, in turn, thanks her for her understanding, and when she comes in early the next morning, there is a small box of chocolates on her desk as a 'thank you'.

No prizes for guessing who is passive (Jane), aggressive (Gina) and assertive (Lisa).

The question is, simply, who gets the best outcome?

Unless you are on a diet, chocolates and a thank-you note sound a better outcome than sitting alone on a chair all night, or bullying someone into submission so that you get what you want but they heartily dislike you for it.

FEATURES OF A PASSIVE COMMUNICATION STYLE

▶ We avoid confrontation at all costs.
▶ We hope people will 'know' what we want without telling them.
▶ We are very concerned with what other people think of us.
▶ We always try to 'please'.
▶ We end up doing things we don't want to.

FEATURES OF AN AGGRESSIVE COMMUNICATION STYLE

▶ We are keen to 'win' always, even at the expense of others.
▶ We are mainly concerned with selfish needs, rather than those of other people.
▶ We get our own way by shouting and bullying, not listening.

Insight

The three main communication styles are Passive, Aggressive and Assertive. You will probably use all three from time to time, but learning to focus on being assertive will get you the best relationship results.

Exercise

Think about your own most used communication style. Do you try to be assertive but struggle? Do you become aggressive, or do you tend to cave in and then feel resentful and fed up?

Which style tends to get you the best results?

Focusing on assertiveness skills

Unless you are aggressive and enjoy it (it does get instant results, but usually at the expense of longer-term relationships) or cave in and prefer the 'peaceful life', you will find that the more assertive you become, the happier you will be and the less stress you will feel at the outcome.

FEATURES OF AN ASSERTIVE COMMUNICATION STYLE

▶ We are keen to find a solution to problems where everyone is happy.
▶ We are strong enough to stand up calmly for own rights.
▶ We are able to accept without rancour that others have rights, too.
▶ We are interested in the other person's point of view.

Two major reasons for choosing to negotiate assertively are:

1 It is usually effective. Quite simply, you are more likely to get the outcome you want.
2 It is the style that others appreciate the most. Therefore, they are less likely to avoid negotiating with you, as they can rely on your remaining calm and looking for a good outcome for both of you.

YOUR RIGHTS

A major feature of assertiveness is that you have the right to say how you feel. The passive person fails to say how they feel at all, and the aggressor will not own their feelings, but will suggest that you 'made' them feel that way. Being assertive means saying, 'I feel very unhappy when you speak to me like that,' as opposed to, 'You make me very unhappy when you speak to me like that.' You are taking responsibility for how you feel, but at the same time, telling somebody that their actions are creating these feelings in you.

STANDING YOUR GROUND

Staying calm and standing firm at the same time takes a lot of practice, but is well worth the effort. In order to do this, you need to keep things simple and operate on a three-step basis:

1 Acknowledge.
2 Use 'but' or 'however' to state how you feel.
3 Offer an alternative solution where you can.

Here's a sample situation:

Jenny's teenage daughter Donna wants to go to a pop concert and stay overnight with her boyfriend. Jenny isn't at all happy about this request. However, rather than simply saying 'no' (and at the very least causing resentment or, at worst, a big row), Jenny acknowledges Donna's request and feelings:

'I appreciate how important and exciting this would be for you, and how much you must be looking forward to it.'

Then Jenny states her own reservations:

'However, I am concerned for you staying overnight as you are only 14, so I am going to say "no" to that.'

Finally, Jenny offers a solution:

'Still, I know you really want to go to the concert, so why don't we arrange for a cab to bring you home at a time that will give you the time to have a drink and a chat afterwards, before leaving?'

Of course, this is in an ideal world of instant compliance. In the real world, Donna would be saying, 'Oh, but Mum…' and continuing to argue her case. Here, you use the 'broken record' technique, which is exactly as it sounds. No matter how Donna pleads, Jenny keeps repeating her terms. She consistently acknowledges what Donna is saying: 'I am sorry that you are so disappointed with my decision', 'I appreciate how cross you are that I am not going along with this' or whatever. Then Jenny will repeat her 'But…' or 'However…' and restate her comments above.

If you use this skill well, sooner or later, the other person will accept your terms and you will both feel happy with the outcome.

We are here only briefly touching on the various skills that will help you develop your assertiveness. You may wish to read further books devoted entirely to this topic, as the more you learn, the better equipped you will become to handle situations in a positive way and achieve a good outcome.

Insight
▶ Becoming assertive means knowing how to express your views and opinions in ways that are not critical of, or offensive to, others.
▶ Standing your ground can be done in a calm and understanding way that means you do not need to 'give way' and yet the other person will also feel that they have achieved a result.

Exercise
A way to practise assertiveness skills is to role play. Perhaps you have a friend, partner or work colleague who might do this with you. You need your partner to be as tricky as possible, while you practise the techniques we have outlined above. Then let them use the same skills on you. You will have fun, and, if you can, get them to agree to practise this regularly until you both feel confident enough to use the skills in 'live' situations.

Avoiding being manipulated

Basic assertiveness skills will take you a long way, but some of those you interact with can be experts in manipulation. Dealing with people who are determined to get their own way can be stressful, especially if this happens on a daily basis.

Here we cover a few of the ways people can attempt to get the better of you, and how you can specifically counter-punch to stay in the winner's corner.

A reminder: Don't forget the broken record technique mentioned in the section above. It is a key skill for preventing people pushing you around.

KEEP A NARROW FOCUS

A key manipulation skill is to widen the argument. One moment you are talking about forgetting to put the rubbish out this morning, and the next minute you seem to be talking about every failing you have had over the last five years. Don't allow this to happen. Draw the discussion back to the specific instance – 'For the moment, let's just talk about what is upsetting you right now' or 'I don't disagree with your points, but let's focus on the present problem.'

LAUGH ABOUT IT

When someone keeps plugging away at a perceived weakness – for example, 'Your spelling is atrocious – there are six errors on the first page alone of this proposal.' A defusing response might be: 'Six errors – my apologies. Let me take it back to correct and I'll give my spellchecker a detention for hopeless work!'

'POOR ME' AND TEARS

Playing a victim is a commonly used manipulation. It can leave you feeling very much the bad guy. Don't be swayed. Acknowledge the emotion with: 'I can see this is upsetting you; however…', then assertively and clearly stay with your point. As with small children, you may be surprised at how quickly this tactic gets ditched once you ignore it.

INTERESTED ENQUIRY

If someone is critical of something that you have done, instead of defending yourself, come right back with something like: 'Exactly what was it about my cleaning the lounge that you believed wasn't good enough?'

Don't take offence – simply take an interested stance on the issue, focusing on your behaviour only.

DELAYING

You can both use this skill and respond to it. You do not need to respond immediately to comments or criticisms, which may lead you to use words you wish you had not, and vice versa. Say: 'I'll get back to you on those points when I've had more time to think about them / obtained further information / talked to Joe Bloggs.' This will give you time to calm down and collect your thoughts.

On the other hand, you may get: 'I'm much too busy to talk about that now.' In this case, say: 'No problem – just give me the best time for you and me to talk and I will come back then.' Don't leave the situation without agreeing a time for further discussion. Use the broken record technique if you get a negative response.

Insight
▶ There is no need to let others get the better of you if you stay calmly assertive and have a toolbox of assertion skills.
▶ The more you use these skills the easier they become and the more relaxed you will feel about dealing with difficult situations. Dread will be replaced by confidence.

Exercise
Earmark someone you have to deal with regularly who can be quite difficult. Decide ahead of time which of the above skills would be appropriate to use, and, when you get the opportunity, give them a go. Make a note of any difference it makes, and whether you feel better for having maintained an assertive stance.

Dealing with threats and abuse

Living with, or working with, others who use aggression in order to get their own way can be very stressful indeed if you do not know how to deal with it. So learning how to defuse another person's threatening or abusive behaviour is an obviously important skill.

We are leaving this aspect of communication until last as we want you to have started developing assertiveness skills before dealing with this.

Insight
If you have not yet mastered your own behaviour, you cannot expect others to have mastered theirs.

Remember:

Rage fuels rage.

The saying 'You cannot win an argument' is simple but true. If you respond to another person's angry outburst by showing anger yourself, neither of you will hear a word that the other says. They will be attacking, you will be defending, and vice versa, like opponents in a boxing ring.

However, when you are being truly, seriously and unfairly attacked you can stand up for yourself. Or, if there is a chance of physical violence, ensure you can escape the situation.

YOU CAN WALK AWAY

If you are uncertain that you will be able to control either your reaction or the situation, then take yourself out of the situation if you possibly can. Then use positive self-talk.

POSITIVE SELF-TALK

Positive self-talk can help to calm yourself down. Maintaining internal hurt, fear or anger will do you no good, so talk yourself through it:

- ▶ 'Jim tends to fly off the handle easily with everyone.'
- ▶ 'I cannot take responsibility for his behaviour.'
- ▶ 'My own anger will pass if I distract myself.'
- ▶ 'I'll take some deep breaths and relax.'
- ▶ 'Why should I let someone else's behaviour affect my own?'
- ▶ 'Being treated unfairly is a fact of life. I will get over it.'
- ▶ 'Retaliation certainly won't help.'

…and many other suggestions of your own. By taking this action, you are defusing your own anger at how you have been treated, rather than attempting to defuse someone else's.

ACKNOWLEDGE THE ABUSIVE BEHAVIOUR

Where you need to stand your ground, don't initially attempt any defence of what is being said to you. To defuse the situation and avoid further confrontation, acknowledging the other person's view (however outrageous and irrational) is a strong response, not a weak one.

'You sound outraged by what has happened' or 'You are shouting really loudly – this has obviously made you hugely angry' will usually take the wind out of their sails somewhat. Bearing in mind that your goal is to calm the other person down, this is an important start.

You may feel like strangling them, but remember – this is all about keeping safe and finding the best outcome.

BE HONEST ABOUT HOW YOU FEEL

If someone is treating you aggressively – especially in a work or domestic situation – tell them clearly how you are feeling. 'I feel quite frightened when you react like that', 'While you are so angry, I don't feel able to talk to you' and 'I am actually concerned that you may become violent' are all valid observations that you have a right to make, to encourage the abuser to take stock of their own behaviour.

OFFER AN APOLOGY (A BACKSTOP)

What?! When I've been treated so appallingly? We appreciate that this may stick in your gullet, but if you are really in fear of someone's violent temper, then holding out an olive branch may be a better solution than ending up with a black eye. This can be more a statement of regret – for example, 'I'm really sorry that what I have done has caused you to get so angry' or 'Can I do anything at all to help you feel better?'

These are not weak responses in these circumstances. They are conciliatory responses that may defuse the situation.

ACCEPTANCE

Simply allowing the angry outburst to wash over you by strongly refusing to engage with the abuser is a positive step. By doing this, you give your assailant nothing to work with. They may keep shouting and abusing you, but, if they get no response, they are wasting their breath and their energy.

AGREE!

Again, What?! Why? Think about it. What could be more 'show-stopping' than being calmly agreed with when you are getting very worked up with and critical about someone? 'You're quite right. I did forget to pay the gas bill / send off the invoice / record the TV programme you wanted.' This response can take the wind out of the sails.

Insight

▶ When confronted with real abuse or threatening behaviour, your goal is to defuse the situation.
▶ Don't discount any means of doing this, even if it goes against the grain. Your further goal is to remain safe and prevent an escalation of abuse or physical violence.

Don't take it personally

One of the reasons that dealing with others can be particularly stressful is that we can take comments and criticisms very personally. For example, if a shop assistant is rude to you, you might believe that a) she has taken a dislike to you, or b) that you have done something to upset her.

How do you feel if a friend says she will call you and does not? Or if someone simply disagrees with a point you are making? These situations are upsetting, of course – we do want our friends to call us, and for people to agree with our opinions. However, any stress that we feel when such things happen will be greatly magnified if we decide that the reason it has happened is due to our own failings or shortcomings.

PERSONALIZATION

Personalization means that you erroneously feel that you are personally to blame for the perceived negative reactions of others: 'If someone disagrees with me, then I must be wrong, and that makes me stupid.' What a very stress-provoking thought that is.

DE-PERSONALIZATION

De-personalizing involves using some of the broader thinking skills we discussed in earlier chapters

▶ Have respect for the opinions of others. There is no rule that says everyone must agree with you, or that, if they don't, you are stupid.
▶ Distinguish between opinion and fact. However strongly either you, or the person talking to you, believe something, that doesn't make it true. There are many different opinions on almost every subject. Opinions are exactly that – simply points of view.

- Have confidence in your own views. You don't need to be right all the time – simply having a view shows some thoughtful intelligence on your part, and you may have valid reasons / past experiences that mean you are more likely to have formed your opinions in a certain way.
- Others have their own problems. The rude shop assistant may have had a row with her boyfriend, the friend who didn't call may have been sick or having family difficulties that she was focusing on.
- Other people suffer from stress as well, and don't always react in the best possible way. This has nothing to do with you.

Use the cricket ball technique

One of the authors worked with a client who was personalizing every criticism his wife made, and it was affecting their relationship very badly. He was a cricket fan and, one day, he came into the office and said:

> *'I can see that personalizing criticism is like letting a cricket ball hit me on the head. It hurts a great deal and leaves a big bump. I now know that I can hold my hand up and catch the ball [the personal criticism] before it hits me. I can then choose what to do with it. I can look at it, play with it, put it down, or even throw it back. But I don't need to let it hit me on the head and hurt me.'*

Insight
- Altercations or criticism can be very stressful. Don't make the stress even worse by erroneously attributing the other person's anger to your personal failings.
- Use thought challenging to work out what might be really going on, and remember to respect others' points of view.

Exercise
Think back over the last week. Can you identify an occasion when you might have erroneously taken something too personally? What went through your mind? Using your diary, jot down some alternative ways of thinking about this, using some of the skills we have mentioned above. How do you feel now?

Communication without words (almost)

Various studies have shown that the words we speak have far less impact than our tone of voice or our body language.

Believe it or not...

- ▶ just 7 per cent of our communication comes from the words we speak
- ▶ 38 per cent comes from our tone of voice, *and*
- ▶ 55 per cent comes from our body language.

If you find that hard to believe, here is a question for you to think about. How would you know, without that person saying a word, if they were:

- ▶ sad?
- ▶ happy?
- ▶ angry?
- ▶ bored?
- ▶ arrogant?
- ▶ interested?
- ▶ uninterested?
- ▶ pleased?

How much is it possible to learn about someone's frame of mind without them actually saying anything? In turn, even when you do not say a word, you are telling people a great deal about what is on your mind!

To stress the importance of the messages you give via your body language, picture this:

> *You walk into a large restaurant, looking for a friend. In the distance you see a couple leaning towards each other across a table. They are speaking, but you cannot hear them. Yet you can (usually) easily tell if the couple are a) being intimate b) arguing c) sharing a joke d) discussing a serious matter.*

All this, without hearing a word they are saying. Bear that in mind.

Remember as a child, when, up in your bedroom, you would hear your mother calling your name up the stairs? All she is calling is your name, yet you could usually tell from that whether a) she was very cross about something or b) tea was ready. Just one word contained a great deal of information on which you would act accordingly.

Now think about your own body language and tone of voice.

You are at a party that you were quite nervous about going to. There are lots of elegant people, and you don't know anyone there except the host and one or two others. You need to start up conversation and get to know a few people. You pick someone to initially approach and chat to. Now write down five things you might do that are non-verbal that would a) show warmth and interest and b) show coolness and lack of interest.

Ensure that your body language and what you are saying match, as your non-verbal communication will give a stronger message than your verbal communication. For example, inviting someone to lunch while continuing to work on your computer will not convey great enthusiasm for the idea. Giving someone some bad news and then walking away in a jaunty, lively manner will suggest you don't really care much about it.

Insight

▶ How you communicate through body language and tone of voice gives a far stronger message than the words you are saying.

▶ Not only can you strengthen what you are saying by using matching body language, you can learn more from others by watching theirs.

Exercise

Have a bit of fun. Create two unimportant situations where you speak to someone, but use body language that does not 'match' what you are saying (you could use one of the examples we gave above).

See what response you get. You might then want to tell the other person what you were testing out, and find out how they felt about the mixed messages. Which did they think was the stronger message?

KEEP IN MIND

1 While we may often feel that it is everyone else who is difficult, obstructive and contributing to our stress, it is a hard task to change the attitudes and behaviours of others. Good communication skills can help us here.

2 If we learn to communicate well, we are more likely to get what we want. A key feature of good communication is to ensure that others understand the point we are making, so learn to be calm and clear.

3 Remember that good communication is not just about talking but about listening and understanding as well. Good listeners tend to have less stress in their lives and generally get on better with other people.

4 We usually feel most 'heard and understood' when someone reflects back to us what we have just said – not simply like a parrot, but with empathy and understanding of the situation that has been described.

5 When we express understanding of another's point of view, we have a much higher chance that they will, in turn, do their best to understand our own angle and this makes resolution an easy possibility.

6 The three main communications styles are: Passive, Aggressive and Assertive. Understand their attributes and be honest with yourself about which of these you use.

7 You will usually find that the more you learn to develop assertive skills, the happier you will be and the less stress you will feel.

8 Avoid being manipulated by being aware of the strategies manipulators use. The broken record technique is an excellent skill for preventing manipulators widening the focus of the debate.

9 Before you can deal with people who are aggressive and threatening, you must have good, assertive communication skills yourself. You cannot expect others to have mastered their behaviour if you have not mastered your own.

10 Remember that non-verbal communication also gives a very strong message and ensure that yours is appropriate to what you are saying. You can also learn a lot from watching the non-verbal communication of others.

Stress at work, stress at home – how to deal with them without losing your job or your marriage

In this chapter you will learn:
- *to assess your stress levels in the workplace and identify your personal stressors*
- *how not to be driven to distraction by distraction*
- *how to keep your relationship in good shape when stress threatens it*
- *a few suggestions for those of you who are stressed-out parents.*

Recognizing stress at work

We discussed earlier in this book the difference between pressure – which is actually good for us – and stress, which is bad for us. In a working environment where we, usually, do not have full control, it is important to recognize any movement from pressure to stress.

We are expected to put up with a certain amount of stress, and are capable of doing so, but if we find ourselves heading towards job burnout, action needs to be taken. The following can be causes of burnout. Do any apply to you?

- ▶ Work overload – you have more to do that you can cope with, and/or deadlines that you find impossible to meet.
- ▶ Work underload – you do not have enough to do, and your job is repetitive and boring.
- ▶ Your hard work is not recognized or rewarded.
- ▶ You are not given the skills to do the job required of you.

- ▸ You work with unco-operative colleagues.
- ▸ You have lack of control over your job that leads to frustration and reduced motivation.
- ▸ You are a victim of bullying or harassment.

Are you coping? First, you need to identify the symptoms that indicate stress.

Answer the following questions:

1 Is your concentration poorer than in the past?
2 Do you feel tired all the time?
3 Has your enthusiasm for your job waned?
4 Does getting up to go to work make you feel depressed?
5 Do you long for weekends/holidays?
6 Do you see your job simply as a means of paying the bills?
7 Are you concerned with your on-the-job performance?
8 Are you relating poorly to your boss?
9 Are you eating or drinking more or less than usual?
10 Have you lost interest in your social life?

As few as three yeses should concern you.

Now you must identify the sources of your stress. Of the following questions, tick those that make you feel stressed and rate them in order of priority (where 10 = stresses me the most):

1 Do you feel that you have far too much to do?
2 Do you feel that you have too little to do?
3 Do you feel you have too much responsibility?
4 Do you feel that you lack authority?
5 Do you work hours far in excess of those in your job spec?
6 Do you find your boss/colleagues difficult to get on with or unhelpful?
7 Do you feel criticized rather than appreciated?
8 Do you feel that there is no relationship between your hard work and the rewards you receive in terms of recognition and salary?
9 Do you feel unable to perform to your best abilities because of the amount of work you must get through?
10 Do you feel less and less able to cope?

You should have now identified a) whether you are suffering from job stress or burnout, and b) which stressors affect you the most.

In the next section we will look at solutions.

Exercise
Use the questions above to identify your stress triggers. Write them down, and add any others that come to mind. You will need to know what to work on specifically in order to reduce the stress you are experiencing.

Work stress solutions

One of the worries employees have when they attempt to reduce stress overload is that they may end up achieving less than they need in order to keep their jobs.

We are mindful that keeping your job is a necessity (unless you decide to change it), but these solutions will make you more productive, not less.

In order to reduce stress at work, you will need to do either one or all of the following:

▶ deal with the specific stressors (get more organized, speak to your boss regarding work overload, speak to the unhelpful work colleague)
▶ challenge your views about your work (that you are not good enough to cope with the challenges, that others don't help you enough, that you get taken advantage of by your boss)
▶ work on being less tense and relaxing more when you are in a stressful situation (use good breathing and relaxation skills, get some fresh air, ensure you eat a healthy lunch).

We have covered all these areas in this book, so be sure that you use them in the workplace when you need them.

Here are some further solutions to workplace stress (including skills we have previously looked at):

SET REALISTIC WORK GOALS

This will incorporate writing down what you can realistically achieve each day, by the end of the week, and, of course, longer-term, larger goals. You will then need to make a time plan to ensure you can achieve these.

LEARN TO NEGOTIATE

When you find yourself in conflict with your boss or your colleagues, you need to negotiate a solution that everyone is happy with. Using the assertiveness skills you have learned, remember to:

▶ acknowledge the other person's position
▶ state your own, and the problem it creates
▶ offer a 'win-win' solution that will hopefully benefit both parties.

(This is more important than insisting totally on what you want, at the expense of the other person.)

LEARN TO DELEGATE

Resist the temptation to do every task yourself. OK – maybe your colleague won't do it quite as well as you, but they will learn. Pass over anything that you feel someone else has the time and ability to deal with.

LEARN TO SAY 'NO'

If you don't have enough time, you don't have enough time. Saying 'yes' to something that you cannot possibly complete to the required standard in the timescale needed will simply cause you further stress. The result may be that your work level will deteriorate, and you produce nothing at all that reflects your abilities – which increases your stress levels yet again.

LIMIT YOUR WORKING HOURS

Working long hours is less productive than you think – as does working without a break. There is nothing clever about missing lunch. The longer we work without a break, the slower our productive output progressively becomes. So we achieve little more than if we work sensible hours and take regular breaks.

IMPROVE YOUR INTERPERSONAL SKILLS

Poor working relationships can cause untold stress – especially in these days of open-plan offices, where many people are thrown together. Make a determined effort to charm even the most difficult colleague – the more people like you, the more they will be willing to help you out and make your own working day easier. Learn not to absorb others' anger and irritation so that you become tense and stressed yourself, when it is actually their problem.

Insight
- ▶ Achieving a reduced-stress or stress-free work environment involves identifying and changing your personal stressors, challenging your negative thinking about events, and working on relaxing your body and ridding it of unwanted tension.
- ▶ You may not be able to address all of these issues, but even working on one will have a positive effect.
- ▶ Think of delegating, saying 'no' more often, checking the realism of your goals, and improving, negotiating and interpersonal skills as well.

Exercise
Pick just one of what are probably several personal stressors in your job. Using the suggestions above, think about what you might do to reduce or eliminate this stressor. Now put your ideas into practice. Check the result. Has it made a difference to your stress levels? If not, you will need to find an alternative solution. But don't give in – keep trying until you make a difference and reduce the amount of stress this problem is causing you.

Knocking workplace stress on the head – away from work

You can do a great deal to relieve work stress outside your place of work. This means making yourself as stress-resilient as possible before you walk through the door.

START YOUR WORKING DAY THE PREVIOUS EVENING

Go to bed in good time. When you work a long day, get home late, and feel cheated out of 'me' time, it is a temptation to grab it back by staying up late. One of the many problems of doing this is that you can eventually get too tired to face going to bed, so you stay downstairs, staring at the TV like a zombie, unable to motivate yourself to climb the stairs. While natural and understandable – don't do it. Set yourself a deadline for going to bed and stick to it, or you will not function well the following day.

GET UP EARLIER

Once you have got to grips with going to bed in good time, why not get up a little earlier? An alarm clock that rings at 7 a.m. is no more of a shock than one that goes off at 7.20 a.m., but an extra tranche of time before you leave for work will ensure that you are relaxed, rather than rushed, when you finally step outside your front door. The good news also is that your body will soon get used to this different timing.

EAT BREAKFAST

'No time.' 'Don't feel like it.' 'I'll grab a coffee on the way in.' When you get up in the morning, your body has gone for many hours without food at all and we recommend that you refuel to give it a chance to support you through the day ahead. Make sure you have something, and that it is fuel-packed – wholegrain cereal, fruit, eggs, orange juice – rather than coffee and a croissant with a sugar content that will actually slow you down rather than speed you up. Give your body a chance.

PHYSICAL EXERCISE

What? Before work? We know – what a horrible thought! However, once you give it a go, you will discover that it wakes you up and makes you feel very energized, rather than tiring you out. There are more opportunities than you think. We are not suggesting an hour in the gym (although you can do this if you like), but possibly walking the dog, walking to work or just getting off the bus one stop earlier and walking the last section. If you drive, could you park a little further away? Do you walk to the railway station? Think about anything you can do to wake your body up with some form of exercise before you sit down in your office. At the very least, do a few minutes of stretching exercises when you get up.

SUNDAY NIGHT STRESS

'Sunday evening blues' is very common. If you suffer from this, make sure that Sunday evening is a relaxing, happy time. Sunday evenings can become stressful because, not only are we acknowledging the end of the weekend and a return to the grind the next day, but we often save up all our unpalatable chores until then – cleaning shoes, ironing clothes, washing our hair, paying the bills. Don't! Make Sunday evenings a haven of pleasure. Cosy up, rent a DVD, plan a nice supper, open a bottle of wine... whatever easy, relaxing pleasure is most enjoyable for you. Begin to look forward to Sunday nights, rather than feel depressed by them as heralding the end of the weekend.

TRAVELLING TO WORK

Far from enjoyable, commuting can be a major stressor. It can mean we arrive at our place of work tired, fractious and already in a bad mood before the working day has started. Think in terms of...

▶ catching an earlier train/bus so that you can enjoy the journey rather than stress about delays

▶ adding a little extra time if you drive to work so that traffic jams are not major stressors

▶ if you are on a train, making sure that you have something to read or listen to that is enjoyable – for example, reading a good novel rather than a financial report

▶ in the car, finding a good radio station or ensure you have a favourite CD with you. Why not get hold of (either purchasing or renting from the library) an audio cassette of a book on your 'to read' list, and listen as you drive?

> **Insight**
> You can make a real difference to your working day by making the non-working part a stress-free zone.

> **Exercise**
> Make a written list using each of the headings in this section, and leave some writing space underneath. Now jot down at least one good idea for a positive change you could make (more, if you wish) in each of these areas. Make sure you start carrying out the changes you have thought of.

Getting the respect you deserve

Being both respected and respectful can have a great impact on a stressful work environment. Many people cite office politics as a huge trigger for stress, often feeling that the backbiting and manoeuvring of others is something outside of their control and yet extremely upsetting.

However, there are a variety of things you can do to generate what we might call a 'respectful environment' that will minimize the stress created via work colleagues. Your focus is to become (if you are not already!) the kind of person others like to have around.

NEVER EXCUSE MISTAKES THAT YOU MAKE

Don't make excuses, and don't point the blame elsewhere. Everyone understands genuine cock-ups (we all make them from time to time) and has respect and admiration for the person who takes full responsibility for what has happened.

GIVE CREDIT WHERE CREDIT IS DUE

Conversely, don't attempt to steal anyone else's thunder. Give credit where credit is due, and praise others' good work, even where it shows up the fact that you did not think of it / do it yourself. No one likes the person who takes credit for something that really was not his or her personal success.

TREAT EVERYONE IN THE SAME WAY

One of the best pieces of advice we could give, with regard to getting on well with the wide variety of people you come across in a working environment, is never treat anyone either as superior or inferior to yourself. If you give everyone exactly the same consideration, interest and respect, from managing director to office junior, you will receive the same respect and consideration back.

DON'T BE A GOSSIP

It is natural to want to chat about the day-to-day goings-on in an office. We are not suggesting that you stand aloof from this. However, don't become part of the office rumour machine, as you will lose the trust and respect of your peers. When chit-chat starts, ensure that you…

- ▶ don't say anything detrimental
- ▶ don't agree with hearsay
- ▶ remain impartial
- ▶ speak up if you know that something said is definitely untrue
- ▶ don't make promises you cannot keep.

It is always tempting to be the 'white knight' who sorts out the problems of others, agrees to meet deadlines that are important, and offers to help all and sundry. However, if you cannot keep your word, your fall from grace will be worse than if you had honestly admitted that you simply could not do this or that.

HELP OTHERS ALONG

Offering to explain something, showing a colleague how to do something they are finding difficult, or simply encouraging anyone who is uncertain of their ability is the sign of a good manager. Taking time from your own work to ensure someone else achieves their own goals (where you have time) will encourage great respect.

LEARN TO LISTEN

Don't be too eager to tell others how to solve their problems. Give them the space and opportunity to talk things through with you first, and to tell you how they feel about whatever has come up. You will be appreciated for listening, and you will have a much better idea of how to resolve issues when you have given time to hear and understand the problem fully.

> **Insight**
> Your work environment becomes a less stressful place if you are both respected and treat others with respect.

> **Exercise**
> One of the most damaging things in the office is the rumour mill. It can be quite hard to resist gossip. Think back over the last week. How did you react when some gossip floated by you? Are you someone who joins in? How could you behave differently in future? How could you help to reduce the gossiping in your office?

Destructive distraction

'It's just impossible to get any work done in my office – there are so many distractions.' This is a common complaint and hugely stressful. On a list of 15 identified workplace stressors identified by managers, distraction and interruption come out as the number-one stressor for busy people under pressure.

QUESTIONS, QUESTIONS

One of the main sources of interruptions to your working day is likely to be other people asking you questions. Look back over the last day or so. How many times did you answer questions from others? How much time did you take to give each answer? If you multiply one by the other, you may get a shock when you realize how much time you give up – in, say, a week – to answering questions from colleagues.

If this is a problem for you, then you need to become disciplined about answering.

SOLUTIONS

One solution – used by many – is a 'free period' each day, where you hang a sign on your door (if you have one) that says, 'Strictly no interruptions, please', or you advise your secretary (if you have one) to hold all calls and not let anyone in.

However, in this day and age, email, texting, faxes and voicemail are all ways of beating the system. So you may need a disciplined formula for answering questions, perhaps along the following lines:

▶ **Questions where the answer lies in print somewhere:** Don't dig around your filing cabinet, or even waste time trying to recall the information the person wants. Simply direct them to the company's policies and procedures, or other manuals, files and resources, and tell the person to find the information themselves.
▶ **Can anyone else answer the question?:** Deflect, deflect, deflect! Tell the questioner who might be able to answer that question for them and leave it at that.
▶ **Monosyllabic responses:** If it is possible to answer a question with a 'yes' or a 'no', do so. Don't elaborate unless it is imperative.
▶ **Economies of scale:** Where you have no choice but to answer fully, be economic. Avoid flannel, avoid being chatty, simply give the information required quickly and clearly.
▶ **Smile:** All of the above solutions will be accepted with grace where you smile at the same time. It will save you from becoming recognized as grumpy and unwilling.

OTHER INTERRUPTION BEATERS

▶ Screen your calls – either via a secretary or an answer machine. Only pick up when relevant and important. Caller ID will let you know who is calling.

- Use email rather than telephoning. The beauty of email is that it is a monologue rather than a dialogue, so you pass over your information without having to answer any questions.
- Learn to screen out noise by using distraction, focusing on what you are doing, or simply humming along with it. Don't allow yourself to become irritated by it, or its annoying characteristics will multiply in your mind.

Insight
- Interruptions are one of the top stressors in an office environment.
- Plan to defeat interruptions and distraction using a variety of skills that will need some practice.

Exercise
What distracts or interrupts you most in your workplace? Having read the ideas above, what can you now do about this to reduce it?

Relationship rescue – when stress strikes it down

One of the casualties of being under stress generally can be the quality of our personal relationships. Develop an awareness of how you react to those you love when you are stressed, and notice whether these reactions become more aggressive and argumentative or whether you become withdrawn and refuse to talk things through at all.

It may even be that your poor relationship skills are the cause of your stress. Do not simply assume that your partner is being difficult. It may be you.

DEALING WITH CONFLICT

All relationships contain elements of conflict, and it is how these are resolved that will decide the quality of the relationship. Under stressful circumstances, you may lose your ability to relate in a loving and mature way. Disagreement is healthy – don't worry about it. Learning the skills of resolution so that everyone feels happy at the end of it is what matters.

INSISTING ON BEING RIGHT

When we feel upset or poorly treated, we often think that a way to feel better is to prove that we're right and that our partner is wrong.

In 'blame mode', you no doubt feel that you are being more than fair, and your partner is being totally unreasonable. In order to prove how right you are, you drag up every piece of evidence you can find to show that your partner is wrong. Why are you doing this? What outcome are you hoping for? Is this a win-win approach?

Think, all the time, in terms of outcomes and results when you are in conflict.

When blaming the other person, are you hoping that they will say something along the lines of, 'I am *so* sorry. I can now see the error of my ways, and how totally right you are. I am completely wrong and cannot apologize enough'?

Does that ever happen? We suspect not.

EFFECTIVE COMMUNICATION

How can you communicate effectively when you are stressed, distressed, upset – and certain you are right? Again, think in terms of outcomes and results. Now please answer the following question (and write your answer down):

Would you rather be right or be happy?

If your answer was 'be happy' (and we are almost sure that it was), then consider the following:

1 If someone raises their voice to you, bullies you verbally, criticizes you rudely, gives you a list of your shortcomings, how do you feel towards the other person? Warm? Understanding? Keen to put things right? Or do you feel that they are rude, overbearing, utterly wrong and deserve to hear a few home truths of their own?

   The answer to this question will tell you how someone else feels about you if you act in an aggressive, blaming way. Thus, the outcome of this mode of behaviour will be poor at best.

2 When engaged in conflict with your partner...

   ▷ be assertive, not aggressive
   ▷ acknowledge their point of view before expressing your own

> ⊳ make it your goal to find a solution that you are both happy with

> ⊳ let your partner speak, and listen attentively. Don't simply wait impatiently for them to stop – or interrupt them – so that you can fire your next shot across their bows.

3 Ask yourself what is likely to happen if you continue to insist on being right and blaming your partner. Your answer will probably be along the lines of: 'We'll end up having a blazing row and not speaking to each other for the rest of the evening.' Then ask yourself if this is the outcome you want.

4 Remember the importance of TONE when you are expressing grievances. What you say may be quite valid. Don't ruin the impact by speaking in such an angry, aggressive way that your partner is immediately on the defensive, and fails to hear the sense in your comments over the attack in your voice. Speak calmly and your partner will listen to what you have to say.

Exercise

In your diary, write down four different communication methods that you use when dealing with conflict with your partner. For example, remaining calm, stating my case clearly, letting my partner express their views – or, on the negative side, getting cross, raising my voice, refusing to listen, walking away.

RELATIONSHIP RESCUE – OWNING YOUR FEELINGS

Relationship problems can cause a great deal of stress. Stress can cause us to react in an angry or inappropriate way to our partner's perceived demands and criticisms. We usually feel, however, that it is our partner who has made us feel angry, upset, unvalued, inferior, perhaps even unloved. We are not to blame for this negative outburst – they made us do it.

For example:

Jim was helping Marie with the housework on Saturday morning. Domestic routine was not Jim's strong point – a messy house was fine by him. So he tended to work without especial enthusiasm, and rather slowly. Marie got crosser and crosser, and more and more critical of Jim's feeble efforts. Eventually, she exploded. 'You make me so angry – you make no effort at all – look at all the mess still in the kitchen you have supposedly tidied.' Jim retaliated with, 'Well, you make me feel useless. You criticize my efforts, you tell me everything I do is wrong. You make me feel like not bothering at all. What's the point?' With that, Jim walked out of the house, leaving Marie fuming and upset – and with a lot of housework now to do on her own.

The problem for Jim and Marie was that each felt that the other one had 'made' them feel as they did – angry in Marie's case; useless and resentful in Jim's.

Insight

Remember this: no one else can make us angry, distressed or resentful – or feel any other emotion. We choose it ourselves.

You may want to argue with this – 'But I really cannot help it', 'It's impossible to control', 'There are limits to what a person can take'. We are not unsympathetic to these views. It can be very difficult to control your emotions – but you do have control. Emotions are not reflex actions, like a knee-jerk or blushing; they are simply responses that we can choose to what extent we activate.

This idea is extremely important, as it stops us from criticizing our partners. There is all the difference in the world between hearing 'You make me so angry when you do that' and 'I feel very angry when you do that', or 'You really hurt me, saying such awful things to me' and 'I feel hurt when you say things like that.'

You are owning your emotions, not blaming the other person for them.

If you practise this, the rewards are enormous. Your partner will not feel criticized or blamed, but will be able to understand your feelings. This will work in exactly the same way if your partner adopts the same ownership of his or her feelings. It becomes safer to be open about how you are feeling, and this type of openness, where there is no blame and no defence, is at the core of real intimacy.

Insight
▶ Owning your feelings means talking about 'I' instead of 'you'.
▶ It means understanding that no one else is responsible for angry outbursts, or the hurtful things that we say. We alone choose whether to get worked up and hostile. We don't have to.
▶ Once we take responsibility for how we feel and react, we can begin to talk more closely to our partner and develop real intimacy.

Exercise
When you have an appropriate, relaxed moment, consider discussing this chapter with your partner. Explain that you are planning to practise rephrasing what you say in order to take ownership of your feelings. Ask them if they would like to try this out as well, so that you can both become used to more constructive dialogue when you have a disagreement or want to explain what is upsetting you.

Stress-free parenting

We appreciate that only a certain number of readers will be parents of young children, and also that dealing with the complex issues of stress-free parenting is more properly addressed in a whole book, rather than in one chapter of a book. However, the following tips will offer a very positive step forward, and you may find that, when your stress levels go down, you will be able to improve your parenting even further without drastic action.

CONSISTENCY

At the heart of good parenting are consistency rules. Children actually prefer a tight framework within which to operate. It makes them feel secure and relaxed – but the framework needs to be the same all the time. Every time you find yourself thinking, 'I can't be bothered to be firm' or 'It's just easier to give in', please don't. If you are consistent, all children learn quickly and easily. Once you abandon that – yes, even just one time – the child learns that he or she can turn the situation around if he or she is willing to fight enough, scream enough, argue enough. It is actually not his or her fault. They are simply learning what the boundaries are. Make sure they are always the same.

CRITICISM

When a child is perpetually rude, untidy, nasty to his or her siblings, throws food around, or any other of the myriad of things that drive you mad, it is easy – and natural – to resort to criticism. 'You are such a badly behaved child', 'No one will like you' and various other harsh words will be on the tip of your tongue. You need, however, to think in terms of what results you want.

For example, Johnny's room looks like a pigsty, and you want him to tidy it up. Not just today, but on a regular basis. Here are two ways that you can put this to him. Which do you think will achieve the best ongoing result?

1 'Johnny, your room is disgusting and so are you. Get upstairs and tidy it straight away or no TV for you tonight.'
   Here, you are giving Johnny the clear impression that you are really angry with him and think he is a messy slob. He's likely to feel resentful and rebellious, and not at all like doing what he's asked.
   or
2 'Johnny, you're usually so neat. It's not like you to have an untidy room.'
   Here, you are giving Johnny the impression that you are proud of his neatness, and quite puzzled by his untidy room. Also you are commenting on his behaviour without labelling him as 'disgusting'. He is more likely to think, 'Hey, Mum thinks I'm neat, so I should attempt to be that way.'

LISTENING AND UNDERSTANDING

Sometimes, our children can behave in a way that leaves us not knowing what to do at all.

For example:

Jenny is taking five-year-old Josh round the supermarket with her. All goes well until he spots some chocolate he really likes. He asks Jenny to buy it for him. When she refuses, on the basis that it will soon be dinner time, Josh starts to make a terrible fuss. Other shoppers stare disapprovingly as they go by. Jenny feels tense and distressed and knows she has a problem on her hands, as Josh keeps up his whining. However, giving in is not an option.

Jenny says to Josh, 'You really want that chocolate, don't you?' Josh stops whining for a moment and nods – wondering if he is going to get his own way. 'And you are very angry because I won't buy it for you, aren't you?' says Jenny. 'Yes,' says Josh crossly, but no longer whining. 'I'm really sorry about that,' says Jenny. 'I know it's your favourite, and I like it too, but dinner will be soon. Why don't I make us some chocolate mousse for dessert when we get home?' 'Yes, chocolate mousse, chocolate mousse!' sings Josh as they head toward the checkout. 'Can I lick the bowl, please?'

Jenny's listening and understanding were far more effective with Josh than shouting, coaxing or giving in. When a parent shows the child that they understand their child's feelings, the child feels soothed by the parent's comfort and concern. They feel nurtured, rather than isolated, and see their parents as understanding allies to whom they can turn for comfort and support.

Insight
▶ Children respond to consistent boundaries, which help them feel secure.
▶ Build praise into constructive feedback, which allows the child to respond positively.
▶ Focus on the behaviour without labelling the child or teenager.
▶ Listening and understanding can often calm a child down when they are upset or demanding.

Exercise
Which of the key skills above do you think you could incorporate into your own parenting style? Give them a go over the next few days, and note the results. Remember that, with children, these may not be immediate if they have been used to different responses, but persevere until you see more positive results.

KEEP IN MIND

1 Stress at work can seem especially hard to deal with, as we often feel we have fewer options to reduce it if we are to keep our jobs. However, severe stress can cause burnout, which could spell the end of your job in any event. So never ignore stress in the workplace or label it as 'going with the territory'.

2 Reducing stress at work involves identifying and changing your personal stressors, challenging your negative thinking about events, and working on relaxing your body and ridding it of unwanted tension.

3 Where you can build some physical exercise into your working day, do so. If you are lucky enough to have a work gym membership, use it. Otherwise, take a walk at lunchtime or cycle to work if you can. You will find that exercise lifts your mood and makes you feel more energized.

4 Ensure that you get enough sleep. When you come home tired from work, it is easy to sit down and feel too tired to get up and go to bed in good time. No matter what is going on around you, set a deadline for going to bed and stick to it. You will feel fresher and more relaxed the next day.

5 Build more time and space into your day. For example, if you usually arrive at work rushed and fractious owing to public transport problems, leave home earlier (it can be done) and catch an earlier train/bus – you may even find yourself with time for a coffee before starting your day!

6 Don't be too keen to solve the problems of others. Let them do this themselves and just be there as a last resource. Listen to their difficulties rather than jumping in with your own solutions. This is less stressful for you and more empowering for them.

7 Learning the skills of conflict resolution is vital in both the workplace and home environments. How you resolve disagreements will decide the quality of your relationship with this person. Poor communication skills actually enhance stress.

8 Remember that no one else can make you angry or upset – you decide this yourself and always have a choice. Learn to manage your own emotions so that you can stay calm in adversity and keep your stress levels low.

9 In close personal relationships, being a good listener is far more effective than being a good talker. To reduce stress in a relationship, make sure that you hear and understand what your partner is saying and then, before you present your own view, acknowledge your understanding of their position by summarizing what you believe they are saying. This gets you both onto the same side of your debate and keeps things calm.

10 If you are a parent, always remember that consistency reduces stress. Where children are confident about boundaries, they feel more secure and you will have far fewer stress-inducing disagreements.

10

Bringing it all together: how to become stress-resilient for good

In this chapter you will learn:
- *the four stages of learning you need to go through to become unconsciously competent at managing stress*
- *how using imagery and visualization can reduce stress and increase your confidence to deal with difficult situations*
- *how good friendships and focusing on others can reduce stress*
- *to see hobbies as stress-busters*
- *about the varieties of outside help available to help with stress relief.*

The four stages of learning – becoming consciously competent

In this last chapter we want to look, with you, at developing stress-resilient habits. Many of them will seem like common sense, but actually incorporating these things into your life might require some effort. Possessing the tools is one thing – using them regularly is another.

There is good news, however. If you make the effort, gradually you will find yourself doing these things naturally. They simply become part of your life.

Have you heard of the four stages of learning? These are the stages that you will need to work through before the positive changes you are making become established parts of your life and you no longer have to consciously think about them to activate them. Don't give up before you reach stage four. Here are the stages:

STAGE 1: YOU ARE UNCONSCIOUSLY INCOMPETENT

This is where you would have been before you even thought of buying and reading this book. You probably accepted your stress as part of your life, and simply tried to cope with it as best you could, without much awareness of the idea of changing things.

STAGE 2: YOU BECOME CONSCIOUSLY INCOMPETENT

This stage is reached when you finally realize that things are not going well, and that you need to make some changes, but you are not quite sure how. You will have been at this stage when you decided to purchase this book.

STAGE 3: YOU BECOME CONSCIOUSLY COMPETENT

We hope that this is the stage you are beginning to reach now. At this point you are making changes, and they are (hopefully) making a difference, but unless you think about them, and focus, they don't happen. This is what being consciously competent means – it doesn't yet happen *naturally*.

This can be the stage at which many people give up. They are finding the efforts required too hard, and nothing happens without a lot of thought and effort. Like the gym membership you used every day, and now rarely bother with, or the diet you started with great hope, but which lasted only until you were offered a chocolate éclair – it's all an effort.

Please stick with it, however, and you will reach...

STAGE 4: YOU BECOME UNCONSCIOUSLY COMPETENT

You're there! No more effort. Suddenly you find yourself doing the things that will allow you to live a relaxed, enjoyable, stress-free lifestyle, and you don't even have to think about it.

This is when it all becomes worthwhile. So keep the four stages of learning in your mind – for everything you attempt that is new requires effort. It will hopefully encourage you to know that the major efforts are temporary, while the change for the better is permanent.

Insight

Understanding the four stages of learning should increase your commitment to making an effort. It will come naturally in the end.

Visualize it!

We think in images more often than we realize. Here is an example:

You have decided to plan your holiday. Sitting in your lounge at
home on a cold February evening, you and your partner browse
through a variety of travel brochures. Suddenly, your partner comes
up with something. 'Listen to this…' they say, and read a description
of the desired holiday out loud to you.

What is going through your mind at this moment? The chances
are, you are visualizing it. You will have pictures in your mind of
white beaches or snowy mountains, and you will almost certainly be
visualizing yourself within this picture – perhaps sipping drinks at a
beach bar, or trekking across a mountain pass.

This is visualization. We use it unconsciously a great deal, and to help
reduce stress, we suggest you learn to use it *consciously*.

For example, perhaps you are feeling unsatisfied in your current job
situation. If you feel that the job is the right one for you, but that
certain areas of it need improvement, you can begin by imagining the
improvements you desire. If, on the other hand, you feel you should
be looking for a new job, then focus on imagining yourself in the new
employment situation you desire.

Insight
Don't get stuck over the terms 'visualizing' or 'imagery'. If you don't see
a completely clear mental image, that is fine. Some people see clear, sharp
images very easily; others simply sense or feel something. We all use our
imagination in different ways – seeing, hearing or feeling being the more
prominent sense for each one of us.

When we are stressed, the images in our mind tend to be negative. We
visualize ourselves failing to cope, being ticked off by the boss, being dumped

by our boyfriend/girlfriend the next time we meet them after a row that we had. It is almost like watching a video in our head – except that it is a video that has not been shot yet, and we are the (very negative) scriptwriters.

Exercise

Here is an exercise (adapted from Cooper and Palmer, 2000) to make visualizing work positively for you. It will help you deal with situations that are worrying you and causing you stress, whether ongoing or in the future.

Give this a go:

1 Think of a future situation that you are stressed about.
2 Think about, or preferably write down, the aspects of the situation that are worrying you the most.
3 Taking each difficulty one by one, think about how you might deal with each of them in a constructive way. It would be sensible to write down your ideas.
4 NOW VISUALIZE THE SITUATION. Imagine each difficulty you are worrying about coming up, and picture yourself coping with it as you have planned.
5 Now repeat the process three or four times until it becomes easier to picture without effort.

Keep this technique in mind and start using it regularly. Become aware of outcomes and how closely they match the visualization you worked on.

If you have a real problem coming up with constructive ways of dealing with your difficulties, ask one or two friends or colleagues how they might deal with the same problem. You will find that everyone has at least one or two solutions to offer, and you can construct your own best answer from these.

Visualization is a powerful tool that can be used in many different circumstances – if you want to win a tennis match, picture yourself playing the winning shot and holding the trophy aloft. If you are going for a work promotion, imagine the boss shaking you by the hand and congratulating you on achieving it. The impact of imagery on your mental state is huge, and it is regarded as one of the most effective stress-management techniques available for dealing with difficult situations.

> **Exercise**
> Think of a stressful situation that you will shortly have to deal with, and use the exercise above to identify the problems and solutions. Then visualize yourself putting the solutions into practice.
>
> Look back at the situation after you have done this. Did you find it less stressful than you had envisaged. Did you achieve a more positive outcome than you had originally expected?

De-stressing by reducing worry and rumination

By worry and rumination, we are referring to the chronic 'niggling away' that goes on in our minds that can seem to override our best intentions to be positive, calm, relaxed, and in control of our lives.

WE'RE DOING EVERYTHING RIGHT, YET...

We read the books, we do the exercises, we incorporate them into our daily routines – and yet, when we climb into bed at night we find that our chatterbox brain goes on chipping away at all of our good work by worrying and ruminating in a chronic, negative way.

You need to understand what worry and rumination are, and why they may need more special attention than classic 'negative thinking' to shift.

HOW WORRY AND RUMINATION DIFFER FROM OUR USUAL NEGATIVE THOUGHTS

We have worked a great deal already with challenging negative thinking and this is an excellent way of reducing stress.

Rumination, on the other hand, tends to be the longer-term, relentlessly ongoing result of specific thoughts. For example, you may hold very specific negative thoughts about a recent situation you think you dealt with very poorly. When you lie in bed at night ruminating, you will generalize this into a longer chain of 'I've never been much good at anything' thinking that is repetitive and self-focused. You will probably go back over all the instances in your life where you have failed – and once you have been through them once, you will go through them again and again until you do finally fall asleep.

Worry is very similar to rumination, with the exception that it tends to be about future events, rather than those in the past. While specific negative thinking can be identified and challenged, generalized worry is like a dog with a bone – it will encompass a myriad of future possible situations and see gloom and doom in all of them.

Are either, or both of these, problems that you have and find difficult to deal with?

To help you cope with worry and rumination, let us find some positive value in them. On the one hand, it can be extremely distressing to focus on personal inadequacies, unrealized goals, relationship worries or other unpleasant matters that threaten our wellbeing. On the other hand, if we simply 'try not to worry' about these thoughts and dismiss them as best we can by replacing them with more positive alternatives, we may be missing an opportunity to review valuable information that can help us identify problems that do need to be addressed.

HOW TO DEAL WITH WORRY AND RUMINATION

You will need to do some written work to get rid of these pests.

If you cannot sleep at night because of these thoughts, or if you have a quiet moment in the day when you recall them, write down as many of them as you can remember. We appreciate that this is no fun and that you may probably rather take an 'out of sight, out of mind' view. Once you have your list, look through it. Put a tick by any thoughts that seem to warrant attention (e.g. 'I really am getting more overweight than ever') and score through those that really have no merit (e.g. 'Supposing I never get a boyfriend?').

Now you can apply constructive thinking to the (hopefully few) thoughts you have been having that you can do something about. You can also use visualization as a good way of ridding yourself of unproductive worry and rumination – simply imagine yourself picking them up off the page and putting them into a waste bin.

You will need to practise the above a great deal before you can 'do it in your sleep', as it were, but your efforts will be well rewarded.

> **Exercise**
> Do you recognize yourself as a worrier or a ruminator? If so, do the exercise above for a few nights and sort out those issues you should be dealing with (helpful information) from those that need to be binned (useless information).

Connecting with others

Being in a state of stress can be isolating. When you feel you have too much to do, and too little time, you tend to focus on practical tasks, ticking them off your list as you race along. Yet one of the best ways of becoming resilient to stress is by connecting more with others.

NURTURE YOUR FRIENDSHIPS

Ask people what they value most in life and it will almost certainly be family and friends. When people have regrets, it is often that they did not do more to nurture friendships and spend more time with the people who mattered most to them.

Research has shown that those with a strong social support system are much more resilient to stress, and better able to deal with stress when it does arise.

What sort of social support system do you have? Below is a questionnaire for you to fill in to give you some idea of whether your support system is strong. Give it a go.

Think of a situation which has caused you a great deal of personal stress. To what extent did each of the following help you with the problem? (1 = little support, 5 = a great deal of support)

▶ Husband/wife/partner
▶ Mother
▶ Father
▶ Sister
▶ Brother
▶ Other relative
▶ Close friend

▶ Work colleague
▶ Doctor/clergy/therapist
▶ Husband – therapist

Add up your total score:

▶ 0–10 = low support
▶ 10–25 = moderate support
▶ 25–40 = high support

Source: Cooper et al. 1998.

How did you score? Do you need to pay more attention to nurturing friendships and support systems? If so, do so. Cultivating friendships can reduce stress, lower your blood pressure and strengthen your immune system. It is even suggested that it may protect you from cancer and heart disease.

What we have not touched on here are pets. Studies show that pet owners suffer less from stress than non-pet owners. So if you really don't have too many friends, then get yourself a cat or a dog.

Insight

Developing and nurturing your social support group will help to keep you stress-resilient.

Exercise

Make a list of those people you could count on to be there for you if you were in difficulties. If the list is not very long, you may need to develop your friendships. Write a list of people you have perhaps lost contact with through not keeping in touch, and put a tick against any friendships that you feel you might like to renew. Now plan to write a letter or make a phone call to at least three of those people over the next month.

DO A GOOD TURN

One of the most common reasons people give for being stressed is lack of time in which to accomplish the urgent tasks of life that need to be accomplished – usually with a tight deadline staring us in the face. The idea, therefore, that one could become less stressed by giving more time to others may not go down too well.

Where we can regard being stressed as equalling being unhappy, it therefore makes sense to assume that becoming happier will equal feeling less stressed. Every piece of research into the conditions required and qualities needed to achieve happiness in life has shown that altruism is always at or near the top of the list. Psychologist Martin Seligman, in his book *Absolute Happiness* (2003), refers to an 'astonishing convergence, across the millennia and across cultures' about this point. The old saying 'What you give, you get back tenfold' stays around for a solid reason.

Doing something for another person can greatly enhance your stress-resilience. Simple acts of kindness and generosity can go a long way.

How come? Well, for starters:

▶ You are less likely to be depressed and will feel more satisfaction with the quality of your life.
▶ The fact that you are contributing to society in some way will give you a more positive outlook generally.
▶ If you decide on regular volunteer work, it gives you a sense of purpose.
▶ Even with little time to give, the sense of doing something worthwhile that gives meaning to our lives beyond simply looking after ourselves is a great stress-buster.
▶ Your sense of self-worth will increase. Stress tends to multiply as our self-esteem reduces. Feeling good about ourselves counteracts this. Liking yourself more, having more respect for yourself and what you are doing with your life, will make you far more stress-resilient.

WHERE DO I BEGIN?

This depends on what you find easiest: either a regular, timed commitment; or simply having more of what we call 'other awareness' – literally thinking more about other people in general and what is going on in their lives, and looking for small ways in which you can help them.

Or you can do both.

If you opt for the former, then bear the following in mind:

▶ Pick something that genuinely interests you – you are more likely to stick with it.
▶ Use your strengths. If you are a reasonable footballer, then offering to help, for example, disadvantaged children learn the game is a better use of your time than delivering food to the elderly.
▶ Where you can involve other family members, it will be more fun – and good for them as well.
▶ Don't overcommit yourself. It is better to 'start small' and be consistent with your contribution, than to give more time and constantly have to cancel a commitment.

Exercise
Spend some time today thinking about what you do for others. Do you consider that you have 'other awareness' to any great extent?

Start listing things that you might do – volunteering at your child's school, for example, or having more contact with a housebound or elderly neighbour. Don't overcommit yourself, but make a start on developing your altruism. In most cases, you will get back more than you give.

What are your hobbies?

Hobbies? I thought this was a book on stress management? Yes, but just a few words on this, please. Becoming stress-resilient means taking time out for the following:

▶ creating a balanced life
▶ having varied interests
▶ ensuring that you build in relaxation time

- ▶ focusing away from stressful thoughts by becoming absorbed in something non-stressful
- ▶ having fun
- ▶ being creative
- ▶ stretching yourself without stress
- ▶ looking to learn new things.

Which all adds up to – hobbies and interests!

What you do is not important as long as it interests you, you get real pleasure from it and feel relaxed when doing it. Some hobbies have a social side – if you are a collector, for example, you may visit exhibitions or belong to a group of like-minded collectors. You might also decide to join a class to learn more about your hobby. Others, like gardening or painting, are highly regarded as very therapeutic because of the still and peaceful environment in which these interests are undertaken. You might, however, prefer something more raucous – becoming a member of a team sport should provide this sort of noisy camaraderie.

Enough said, but do take this seriously. Consider how you spend your spare time, and whether becoming actively involved in something new that would provide pleasure and absorption could add to your life.

Insight

Hobbies and interests are excellent stress-busters.

Exercise

Do you already have one or more hobbies or interests? If you do, well and good. If you don't, jot down a few possibilities. Brainstorm some ideas and then review them. Is there anything in the list that you might like to give a go? Give consideration to what spare time you have, whether you like sedentary things or racing around, whether you prefer social hobbies or quiet solitude. Now pick one and write a brief action plan for how you are going to get started.

Cultivating calm

Occasionally, reducing your stress levels in a way that involves very little is a necessity. While we encourage you to learn various skills, techniques and lifestyle changes that will make a real difference to your stress levels, we acknowledge that sometimes the very idea of *thinking* your way out of stress is just not what you can face at that moment.

Stress + Tiredness = Requirement for a Peaceful Place

FIND A SANCTUARY (OR TWO)

If you do not already have at least one place in your home – and possibly at work – that you can escape to when the demands on you and pressures around you are too great, then create one.

'But there is nowhere to go' – well, think about it. You will have a bedroom and a bathroom – and possibly a guest room. How often do people actually stay? Replace the bed with a sofa bed and you are ready to create your own oasis.

If you are female (or possibly male), you may have had a beauty treatment at a spa. Usually, the room that you are shown into while you wait for your massage, pedicure or whatever is an oasis of tranquillity. You can achieve the same easily at home. Some low lights, a few candles, soft music, a comfy chair or sofa. There is nothing more to it.

TAKE A BATH

When we rush to get going in the morning, a quick shower is far more time-effective than a bath. But it can become a habit. When did you last take a bath? This is not about getting clean – this is about total relaxation in an oasis of calm.

▶ If you are in a family environment, book the bathroom for half an hour ahead of time, and tell everyone that they are not to disturb you.

- Make sure you have loads of hot water, a big fluffy towel and all the bath oils, soaps, face masks, eye masks, goat's milk treatments, etc., that you need.
- Turn off the bright light. Light half a dozen candles. Bring in a CD player and your favourite relaxing music.
- Lie back and close your eyes.

This is so simple, yet few of us do it – which is why we mention it here.

REALLY CAN'T STAY AT HOME?

Too noisy, too cramped, too many people, phone calls, pets, etc.? Have you ever been to your local park? Do you live within striking distance of a coffee shop or a bookshop that has those lovely squidgy settees to sit on? Start thinking – you may have other local oases-away-from-home that will give you those chilled-out, peaceful moments that you need.

> **Exercise**
>
> If you don't already have a sanctuary of any sort, now is the time to give some thought to making or finding one. Could you use any part of your home? What alterations would you need to make to achieve this? Where can you take time out in the workplace?
>
> Unless this is anathema to you, plan a long, hot, scented bath for your next free evening. Nip out to the candle/aromatherapy store and stock up first. Really relax and enjoy it – and then plan your next one.

Take a break

While this is an obvious stress-beater for some, the number of people who say 'I am just too busy to take a break' or 'When I go away, all I think about is work, so there seems little point' are myriad.

Are you one of these? If not, move on; but if you are, let us encourage you to think again.

PRE-PLANNING

For busy, stressed people, holidays only happen with pre-planning. If you are someone who says 'As soon as I see a free window, I'm off', it won't happen. You may need to plan far ahead, but plan.

Don't say 'I just like to do things at the last minute.' This can mean 'never'. Also, for stress reduction, one of the joys of a break is not just the being on it, but the looking forward to it. Knowing that you are going skiing / sitting on a beach in five months' time will get you through that period in a more positive way. We all work much better when we can see an end in sight – in this case a holiday. So again, we urge you – plan ahead.

WITH WHOM?

Some of you will have families and friends as travelling companions. However, we meet many people whose main reason for not going away is 'No one to go with'. Join a group! This can be an interest group – painting, sailing, hill walking – or a singles group – many tour operators offer singles holidays in age groups, so that you will not be the only under 30 or over 60. Yes, it can be daunting to show up on your own at the airport / train station – but remember, it is the same for everyone, and this will be an excellent opportunity to make new friends.

WHERE?

Having built-in travelling companions makes whom to go with easy, but where to go more difficult. Keep a file through the year of places you read about, or a neighbour, friend or work colleague tells you about, so that you have always got a choice of places you want to go to and see. This gives you much more chance of agreeing something with your partner than having only one destination in mind – which may not be their first holiday choice at all.

Be flexible – there is always next year.

MINI-BREAKS

For those who really do find it hard to relax away from work for more than a few days, the idea of mini-breaks has really taken off.

Taking a break from Thursday to Monday usually means people hardly notice you are not there, which makes it much easier to get away.

For the most stress-reducing breaks, consider the following:

▶ A spa weekend. Look in the paper for bargain breaks – spa hotels love you at weekends when all the businesspeople have gone, and this is reflected in the lower prices.
▶ You may groan but walking holidays are excellent de-stressors. Plan your own, or get in touch with a company that plan walking tours. They are excellently organized, with leaders to meet you at regular intervals en route and to ensure your hotels are sorted out for you. Again, they are an opportunity to make new friends as well.
▶ A weekend either on or close to water is hugely relaxing. Either hire a boat, or stay by a lake and walk, sail, row or paddle. Go to the seaside out of season. Some resorts are far more beautiful and restful at these times.
▶ Painting breaks are renowned for their therapeutic qualities (even if you cannot paint at all – it really doesn't matter, and you will learn).
▶ Head off to the countryside and stay in a pretty inn.
▶ Continental weekend city breaks are fascinating. List the cities you would like to explore – Prague, for example, is wonderful – and book a trip. You will feel as though you have been away for far longer than two or three days.

> **Exercise**
> Do you have any holiday plans? If not, make a plan right now, today, for at least one long weekend away within the next 12 weeks. Give some thought to the one after that as well, so that this becomes a regular feature of your year, not just a one-off. Write your plans down and show them to someone. Ask that person to check back with you regularly to see that you are activating this.

Developing a sense of perspective – knowing what is really important

Stress is often the result of not achieving the things we feel are important.

What we consider to be important is very much the product of our personal values and attitudes. However, we often give little or no time to considering what these are. We often inherit our parents' views rather than develop our own.

If we find our lives full of stress and unhappiness, we need to review our sense of perspective. What are we trying to achieve in our lives? Is this consistent with the values and attitudes we have? Do we need to make changes so that there is a correlation between the two?

James's story

James grew up in a family that valued financial success above all. His father was a successful banker and assumed that James would follow in his footsteps. James was always urged to try harder, to win at everything, and to be exceedingly competitive. He did well at school and university, and his father pulled strings to get James a job in the City. Earning a high salary, James worked exceedingly long hours under stressful circumstances – and thoroughly disliked his life.

After a while, James started going out with a woman who was a social worker. Her values – that caring for others was more important than a high salary – began to make James think more about this. The more James saw what a happy, balanced life his girlfriend had, the more frustrated he became with his own stressful existence, and the harder it was to cope with his life as it was.

James took some time to review his life, and to look at his own values – as distinct from those his parents had instilled in him. He realized that he did not automatically share his father's views, and, while he respected them, the fact that they were not his own values was causing most of the stress in his life.

James decided to give up banking and went to help a friend run a bookshop, eventually opening one of his own. When he married and had his own family, he ensured that his children were able to develop values of their own, and to decide for themselves what was important in their lives.

We hope that James's story gives you the message. You need to clarify what your values are, and look at whether you are achieving what to you is important. Do this test to get an idea of what really matters to you:

Questionnaire: What are your values?

Rate the following statements from 0–3, where 0 = 'not important at all to me', and 3 = 'extremely important to me':

1 Achieving financial success.
2 Being the best at things I do.
3 Looking good physically.
4 Having a close family.
5 Others seeing me as successful.
6 Others seeing me as kind and trustworthy.
7 Having lots of friends.
8 Having total control at work.
9 My children being high achievers.
10 Spending some of my time helping others.
11 Having plenty of time to relax.
12 Having hobbies and interests outside work.

Look at the statements you gave 3s to. This will tell you a great deal about your values.

The important question to ask yourself now is: 'Is my way of life in line with my values?' If your answer is 'no', here is another cause of your stress.

You need to make changes now, to ensure that the life you are living is consistent with the values you most believe will bring you happiness.

Insight
▶ Your values and attitudes play a large role in determining your stress levels.
▶ To become stress-resilient, your lifestyle and your values need to match as closely as possible.

That's funny – appreciating humour

That laughter is the best medicine is well known. However, most of the time, when stressed, harassed, rushed and anxious, we simply forget about it. There simply doesn't seem very much to laugh about.

This isn't actually true. Many of the hassles and inconveniences of life offer you the option of either driving yourself insane over them or seeing their funny side. It simply requires looking at things hard, and in a certain way.

DON'T BE TOO SERIOUS

Taking life too seriously is a mistake, unless you want your stress levels to rise. Humour will increase your stress-resilience and enable you to relax a lot more.

Much stress comes from giving too much importance to how you see yourself. Find a funny side to defuse difficult situations and you will get others laughing with you.

HUMOUR AS GOOD MEDICINE

Humour will…

▶ relax your body
▶ increase your immunity
▶ give you a calmer, more positive perspective.

BUT LIFE IS SERIOUS – WHERE CAN I FIND ANY HUMOUR IN IT?

▶ Laugh at yourself more – become self-effacing. Telling things in a way that makes you look slightly idiotic is both endearing, and gives others a chance to laugh with you. This really is a quality to cultivate.

▶ Spend more time with funny people and notice what they find funny, how they tell stories, what they do in general to make others laugh.

▶ Start a humour scrapbook. Whenever you read anything funny in a newspaper or magazine (*Reader's Digest* is an excellent source of humorous anecdotes), cut it out and stick it in your book. When you hear a funny joke, record the punch line. You never know, you may even recall it at a good moment.

▶ Start a collection of films or TV series that have really made you laugh. Watching professionals using humour is an education in learning it yourself.

Exercise
When did you last have a really good laugh? Why? If you are not someone who normally laughs at yourself, jot down in your diary two or three recent occasions where things went wrong for you. Now ask yourself whether you could retell these disasters, putting a humorous spin on them? Get used to asking yourself this question and it will soon come naturally to you to make a comedy out of a crisis.

When going it alone is too tough – seeking outside help in stress reduction

Sometimes, in spite of our best efforts, we feel the support of outside professional assistance of some sort or other may be an answer to relieving stress symptoms. Such external assistance can take the form of physical relaxation, alternative therapies or psychological therapies. All have their place, and you need to consider which is the best for you – possibly by trying different therapies out, or asking for suggestions from friends and colleagues who have tried them.

PHYSICAL THERAPIES

Massage
When it comes to alleviating stress – at least for a period of time – massage rates very highly. Try it. If it works for you, try to make it a regular event. Its virtues as a de-stressor are many:

▶ It will help you sleep better.
▶ It can boost your immune system.
▶ It reduces the hormones that encourage stress.
▶ It increases serotonin levels – the 'feel good' brain chemical.
▶ It can reduce your blood pressure.
▶ It feels blissful while you are having it!

Yoga
We hardly need reiterate the benefits of yoga, which will probably already be well known to you. Through movement, breathing and body control, yoga helps you to relax and relieve stress. It is said that just 15 minutes of yoga a day can enable you to feel more relaxed, concentrate better and sleep more soundly. Definitely worth a try!

ALTERNATIVE THERAPIES (A SMALL SAMPLE)

Acupuncture
Practised in Asia for more than 5,000 years, acupuncture aims to release the flow of energy that can be blocked by stress. It is a therapy now recognized by the World Health Organization, and there is a growing body of evidence that its healing powers for a variety of ailments, including stress, are considerable.

Reflexology
Reflexology advocates that the underside of your foot is a miniature representative of your body as a whole. Working with a detailed diagram that relates areas of the foot to areas of the body, the reflexologist manipulates the foot, working to both soothe and relieve the corresponding troubled area of your body.

Cranial osteopathy
The focus of cranial osteopathy is to apply light pressure to the head and body to encourage the release of stress and tension and to encourage a relaxed state of mind and body.

Aromatherapy
Scents really do make a difference. Aromatherapy has been used throughout history in the East, and is now gaining wider acceptance in the Western world. Aromas work because they trigger the brain to release neurotransmitters (chemical messengers), which control blood pressure, breathing, heart rate… and stress levels. While you have the option of visiting a professional aromatherapist, most health food stores sell a variety of essences that you can use at home, if you prefer.

PSYCHOLOGICAL APPROACHES

Counselling and psychotherapy
Stress can often be induced, or made worse, by crises in your life that you find hard to deal with–for example, by divorce, redundancy, bereavement or other personal difficulties, or by past events (possibly even in your childhood) that you have not dealt with and moved on from, such as feelings of low self-esteem caused by overcritical parents.

Talking these issues through with a therapist who can help you come to terms with the past (usually called insight-based therapy) or who will help you discover solutions to your difficulties through changes you might make in your present thinking or circumstances (solution-focused therapy) may enable you to eliminate the stress associated with these problems.

Life and personal coaching
Where you feel that your stress is caused more by simply not being in control of your life, where you feel stuck in a rut that you cannot seem to get out of or where you really don't know what the best changes would be to make to your life, then life or personal coaching will be able to help you.

This is a goal-oriented approach, where the coach will help you to ensure that you make the best decisions to rebalance your life and reduce stress by helping you define your goals and then work with you to encourage you and to ensure that you achieve them. In a sense, the coach is helping you to define more clearly what you want, and also to develop order out of chaos, both of which will result in a huge decrease in your stress levels.

Insight
▶ There is a wide variety of professional help available to relieve stress, both physical and psychological.
▶ You may want to try two or three to see which helps you the best.

Exercise
Have you ever considered – or tried – any of the therapies that we have discussed above? If not, in the light of knowing how helpful they can be in reducing stress levels, are there any that you would be willing or interested in trying out now? We suggest you research two or three, then pick one (only) and book an appointment to try it out.

The mayonnaise jar and two cups of coffee

When problems in your life seem almost too much to handle, when 24 hours in a day are not enough, remember the mayonnaise jar and two cups of coffee. There are many variations of this story, and you may already be familiar with them, but the point is still powerful, and worth making. A professor stood before her philosophy class and had some items in front of her. When the class began, without saying a word, she picked up a very large and empty mayonnaise jar and proceeded to fill it with golf balls. She then asked the students if the jar was full. They agreed that it was.

The professor then picked up a box of small pebbles and poured them into the jar. She shook the jar lightly. The pebbles rolled into the open areas between the golf balls. She then asked the students again if the jar was full. Again, they agreed that it was.

The professor next picked up a box of sand and poured it into the jar. Of course the sand filled up everything else. She asked once more if the jar was full. The students responded with a unanimous 'yes'.

The professor then produced two cups of coffee from under the table and poured the entire contents into the jar, effectively filling the empty space between the grains of sand.

The students laughed.

'Now,' said the professor, as the laughter subsided, 'I want you to recognize that this jar represents your life. The golf balls are the important things – your family, your children, your health, your friends and your favourite passions – things that, if everything else was lost and only they remained, your life would still be full. The pebbles are the other things that matter, such as your job, your house and your car. The sand is everything else – the small things. If you put the sand into the jar first,' she continued, 'there is no room for the pebbles or the golf balls.'

The professor went on: 'The same goes for life. If you spend all your time and energy on the small things, you will never have room for the things that are important to you. Pay attention to the things that are critical to your happiness. Play with your children. Take time to get medical check-ups. Take your partner out to dinner. Play another 18 holes of golf. There will always be time to clean the house and mend the broken chair. Take care of the golf balls first – the items that really matter. Set your priorities. The rest is just sand.' One of the students raised her hand and inquired what the coffee represented. The professor smiled. 'I'm glad you asked. It just goes to show you that no matter how full your life may seem, there's always room for a couple of cups of coffee with a friend.'

Exercise
Take a quiet moment to spend five minutes doing this test.

You get some bad news. You are told that you only have a few months to live. Now, what will you miss the most? Perhaps seeing your children grow up? Perhaps the blue sky and the countryside around you? This will give you an idea of what is really most important to you.

Write these things down. Now write down all the things that have caused you stress in the last week, and put ticks against the ones that seem to really matter, in the light of the above.

We hope you have very few ticks!

And finally... balance your life!

To have a truly stress-resilient life style, you need to ensure that you have a balanced life with variety in it. We have constructed a questionnaire for you below, which will show you whether you have enough balance in your life.

Questionnaire: How balanced is your life?

Tick those which apply to you:

1 I enjoy my work but don't work ridiculous hours.
2 I have at least one or two hobbies and interests that I enjoy.
3 I have great friends and see them regularly.
4 I have a supportive family.
5 I take at least one holiday each year.
6 I spend some of my time helping others.
7 I don't have particular money worries.
8 I have strong religious/spiritual beliefs.
9 There are always two or three things in the week that I really look forward to.
10 I love trying new things and meeting new people.
11 I see the funny side of most things.
12 I consider my life to be fairly well balanced.

If you have ticked less than four of the above, you don't really 'have a life' in the best sense of the phrase. You will need to work hard on adding more variety to your life if you are to become truly stress-resilient.

If you have ticked four to eight, there is room for improvement. Look again at those points you have failed to tick and think about how you might incorporate them into your life.

If you have nine to 12 ticks, then you have a balanced life and there is little more for you to do other than to enjoy it!

If you scored poorly, focus on areas that you can change or incorporate into your lifestyle. Understand the importance of becoming stress-resilient, and ensure that you aim to achieve nine 'ticks' on the chart above within six months.

KEEP IN MIND

1 Bear in mind the four stages of learning and do not give up on the changes you wish to make until you reach Stage 4.

2 Visualization – seeing something as an image rather than as a thought – is a powerful tool. Use it to picture positive outcomes. The impact will be great: imagery is a very effective stress-management technique.

3 If chronic worry and rumination are a problem for you, don't simply 'try not to worry' (that which we resist persists) but replace your negative thoughts with more positive alternatives that may help you to actually address your problems rather than simply worry about them.

4 Nurture your friendships. Research has shown that those with a strong social support system are much more resilient to stress.

5 Altruism – being helpful to others – has been constantly proven to be the biggest mood-lifter but also the least used. Find time to do something for someone else: simple acts of generosity can go a long way.

6 Hobbies and interests are excellent stress-busters.

7 Create a calm, quiet space for yourself and discipline yourself to take the time to use it – for meditation or simple relaxation.

8 Take time to think what is really important to you. You may find that you need to review your values in order to work out what will bring you real, long-term happiness and contentment. Then ask yourself whether the way you are living your life now is in line with your values. If it isn't, change it.

9 'Laughter is the best medicine.' Use it to reduce stressful situations and bolster your immune system.

10 Where you still struggle, even after having worked hard to reduce your stress yourself, don't dismiss or underestimate getting professional help. There are a wide variety of options, both physical and psychological, so work out which might suit you best.

Taking it further

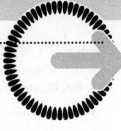

Seeking professional help

If you are feeling very stressed and you have done your hardest to eliminate these difficulties on your own with only partial success, you might wish to consider professional assistance.

Psychological therapy can be very helpful in this regard. In this book, we have taken a Cognitive Behavioural and Rational Emotive Behaviour Therapy approach. If these approaches appeal to you, then you might wish to work with a qualified therapist who is accredited by either the Association for Rational Emotive Behaviour Therapy www.arebt.org or the British Association for Behaviour and Cognitive Psychotherapies www.babcp.org.uk. These two professional bodies maintain an online register of accredited therapists. Coaching can also be useful where you feel stuck in a rut, as it is a goal-oriented and motivational approach. The CBT Register UK (www.cbtregisteruk.com) and the Centre for Coaching (www.centreforcoaching.com) maintain registers of qualified therapists and coaches.

References and further reading

Bilodeau, L., *The Anger Workbook* (Center City, MN: Hazelden, 1992).

Butler, G. and Hope, A., *Managing Your Mind* (Oxford: Oxford University Press, 1995).

Clegg, B., *Instant Motivation* (London: Kogan Page, 2000).

Cooper, C. and Palmer, S., *Conquer Your Stress* (London: CIPD, 2000).

Covey, S., *The Seven Habits of Highly Effective People* (London: Simon and Schuster, 1992).

Davis, M., Eshelman, E. and McKay, M., *The Relaxation and Stress Reduction Workbook* (Oakland, CA: New Harbinger, 2000).

Doherty, W., *Take Back Your Marriage* (New York: Guildford Press, 2001).

Dryden, W., *Dealing with Difficulties in REBT* (London: Whirr, 1996).

Dryden, W., *Overcoming Procrastination* (London: Sheldon, 2000).

Dryden, W., *Progress in REBT* (London: Whirr, 1992).

Elkin, A., *Stress Management for Dummies* (New York: Wiley, 1999).

Gillen, T., *Assertiveness*, (London: CIPD, 1997).

Goleman, D., *Emotional Intelligence* (London: Bloomsbury, 1996).

Hargreaves, G., *Stress Management* (London: Marshall, 1998).

McMahon, G., *Coping with Life's Traumas* (Dublin: Newleaf, 2000).

Namie, G. and Namie, R., *The Bully at Work* (Naperville, IL: Sourcebooks, 2003).

Padesky, C., *Mind over Mood* (New York: Guildford, 1995).

Palmer, S., 'The Negative Travel Beliefs Questionnaire (NTBQ)', *The Rational Behavioural Therapist* 7/1 (1999), pp. 48–51.

Palmer, S. and Cooper, C., *How to Deal with Stress* (London: Kogan Page, 2010).

Palmer, S., Cooper, C. and Thomas, K., *Creating a Balance* (London: British Library, 2003).

Potter-Efron, R., *Angry All the Time* (Oakland, CA: New Harbinger, 2004).

Robinson, J., *Communication Miracles for Couples* (Boston: Conari, 2000).

Ross, J., *The Mood Cure* (London: Thorsons, 2003).

Seligman, M., *Authentic Happiness* (London: Nicholas Brierley, 2003).

Seligman, M., *Learned Optimism* (New York: Free Press, 1998).

Wells, A., *CBT of Anxiety Disorders* (Chichester: Wiley, 2000).

Wilding, C. and Palmer, S., *Beat Low Self-Esteem with CBT* (London: Hodder Education, 2010).

Index

Credits and acknowledgements

Front cover: © Julián Rovagnati–Fotolia

Back cover: © Jakub Semeniuk/iStockphoto.com, © Royalty-Free/Corbis, © agencyby/iStockphoto.com, © Andy Cook/iStockphoto.com, © Christopher Ewing/iStockphoto.com, © zebicho/Fotolia.com, © Geoffrey Holman/iStockphoto.com, © Photodisc/Getty Images, © James C. Pruitt/iStockphoto.com, © Mohamed Saber/Fotolia.com

The publisher and authors would like to thank the authors and/or publishers for their kind permission to adapt or re-use the following:

Stress responses questionnaire (Chapter 2) and visualization exercise (Chapter 10): C. Cooper and S. Palmer, *Conquer Your Stress* (London: CIPD, 2000); Beliefs indicator test (Chapter 3): S. Palmer, 'The Negative Travel Beliefs Questionnaire (NTBQ)', The *Rational Behavioural Therapist* 7/1 (1999), pp. 48–51; Social support questionnaire (Chapter 10): C.L. Cooper, R.D. Cooper and Lynn H. Baker, *Living with Stress* (Harmondsworth: Penguin, 1988).